AFRICAN AMERICAN TRAVEL NARRATIVES FROM ABROAD

AFRICAN AMERICAN TRAVEL NARRATIVES FROM ABROAD

Mobility and Cultural Work in the Age of Jim Crow

GARY TOTTEN

UNIVERSITY OF MASSACHUSETTS PRESS
Amherst and Boston

Printed in the United States of America

ISBN 978-1-62534-161-7 (paperback); 160-0 (hardcover)

Designed by Sally Nichols
Set in Adobe Garamond Pro
Printed and bound by Maple Press, Inc.

Library of Congress Cataloging-in-Publication Data
Totten, Gary.
African American travel narratives from abroad : mobility and cultural work in the age of Jim Crow / Gary Totten.
pages cm
Includes bibliographical references and index.
ISBN 978-1-62534-161-7 (pbk. : alk. paper) — ISBN 978-1-62534-160-0 (hardcover : alk. paper)
1. American literature—African American authors—History and criticism. 2. Travelers' writings, American—History and criticism. 3. Travel writing—History—19th century. I. Title.
PS153.N5T666 2015
810.9'896073—dc23

2014050124

British Library Cataloguing-in-Publication Data
A catalogue record for this book is available from the British Library.

For Christine, Nicolas, Peter, and Anne

CONTENTS

ACKNOWLEDGMENTS

I am grateful to a number of individuals and institutions that supported this project, supplied materials, and provided insights. Colleagues at North Dakota State University helpfully discussed various aspects of the book during its writing, and graduate and undergraduate students in my travel writing and African American literature courses willingly explored with me the ideas and texts that shaped my arguments here. I also benefited from the excellent work of my graduate assistants Justin Atwell, Steven Hammer, and David Lemke.

Many of the ideas in the book were initially presented at conferences of the American Literature Association, International Society for Travel Writing, and Modern Language Association. Questions and feedback from colleagues and audience members at these conferences were invaluable during the writing process. Brian Halley, my editor at University of Massachusetts Press, has been most encouraging and patient from proposal to finished manuscript. I also appreciate the work of the editorial staff at the press including Carol Betsch, Mary Bellino, and Amanda Heller, who guided the project through the publication process, as well as excellent revision suggestions from anonymous reviewers. The staff of the North Dakota State University Library, Beinecke Rare Book and Manuscript Library at Yale University, and New York Public Library have provided excellent assistance in locating and obtaining sources. Finally, I could not have completed the project without the support and good humor of my wife, Christine, and my children, Nicolas, Peter, and Anne.

An earlier version of chapter 1 appeared in *African American Review* 42, no. 1 (2008): 47–60. An earlier version of chapter 2 appeared in *MELUS* 32, no. 2 (2007): 107–31.

AFRICAN AMERICAN TRAVEL NARRATIVES FROM ABROAD

INTRODUCTION

In her autobiography, *Crusade for Justice,* Ida B. Wells describes her response to a minister who had unjustly accused her of immoral behavior. She demanded that he read a retraction of his remarks from the pulpit and notes that she "wanted him to know at least one southern girl, born and bred, who had tried to keep herself spotless and morally clean as [her] slave mother had taught [her]."[1] Accusations of unseemly conduct followed Wells throughout her life,[2] and to counter such attacks, she would often refer to herself in her travel essays as virtuous and womanly. In accounts of her 1893–94 antilynching tours in the United Kingdom, Wells emphasizes her respectability and femininity and links these characteristics to her experience in the segregated South, specifically to episodes in which her gender and morality were attacked by those wishing to enforce the segregation and potential lynching of her black female body. Visual images of black bodies play a significant role in Wells's narratives and travels. An image of her own face on the cover of her antilynching pamphlets, for example, served as an assertion of subjectivity meant to counter the dehumanizing acts described within, and she often depicted the horrific physical realities of lynching to her U.K. audiences, at one meeting circulating a graphic photo of the lynching of C. J. Miller.[3] Wells's deployment of positive and negative images of the black body, both her own and others', not only certifies black moral character but also exposes the irrationality of lynch law and the horrors of segregation and racial violence in the United States.

Several decades after Wells's antilynching tours, Zora Neale Hurston traveled to Haiti and Jamaica to study religious practices in the West Indies, and in 1938 she published *Tell My Horse,* an account of her travel and fieldwork. In her narrative Hurston emphasizes her control over information about herself and her research agenda. For example, she visits the Maroons at Accompong, Jamaica, ruled by a Colonel Rowe, and though she senses that he has questions about the motives behind her visit, she does not reveal to him what they are. He offers to stage a dance for her, but she declines, not telling him that she is "too old a hand at collecting [ethnographic information] to fall for staged-dance affairs."[4] In both cases she emphasizes her expertise and control over her work and identity and links her physical and professional mobility to her acquisition of cultural knowledge.

Hurston's ethnographic methods rely on both the mobility and the stasis of the black female body. As an interesting counterpoint to her mobility as a traveler, soon after her arrival in Haiti in 1936, Hurston notes in an undated letter to Henry Moe, her mentor at the Guggenheim Foundation, that her approach is to "just squat down awhile" and wait for things to happen.[5] At other times Hurston asserts her subjectivity and emphasizes her mobility through the degree to which she physically participates in Haitian cultural practices. Her role as a participant observer, even as an initiate observer as she goes through a Canzo ceremony (the penultimate step toward the voodoo priesthood), provides her with an impressive degree of firsthand access to voodoo and its adherents.[6] She privileges her own eyewitness experience of the ceremony and its actual practice over the scholarly explanation of it. Yet despite her physical immersion in Caribbean cultural practices, she is careful to emphasize that she has not been converted to voodoo in a way that would compromise her objectivity or professional authority.

These experiences from the travel writing of Wells and Hurston highlight the diverse cultural work of the African American travel narrative in the age of Jim Crow. Wells participates in the circulation of black bodies, both literally and visually, in her travel, travel narratives, and photographs and thus speaks truth to the lies of racial violence. Hurston's narrative negotiates the discursive space between the authority of the participant and the distanced objectivity of the professional. Both travelers undertake cultural work relating to issues of identity and mobility and call our attention to the ways in which late nineteenth- and early twentieth-century African American travel narratives reflect *and* intervene in their cultural moment.

I begin and end this book with Wells and Hurston because their travel narratives bracket a particularly tumultuous but significant period in

African American travel discourse and culture. Wells's late nineteenth century represents an important moment in the history of African American travel writing, a time when African Americans are more mobile both within the United States and abroad but also more limited by increasing racial violence, which Wells documents in her antilynching pamphlets *Southern Horrors: Lynch Law in All Its Phases* (1892) and *A Red Record: Tabulated Statistics and Alleged Causes of Lynchings in the United States, 1892–1893–1894* (1895).[7] Wells's travel essays in the *Chicago Inter-Ocean* newspaper, describing her antilynching tours in the United Kingdom, call attention to both the opportunities for increased movement and the constraints that racial violence places on African American mobility.

Zora Neale Hurston's *Tell My Horse* was published near the end of the Harlem Renaissance, a period of artistic revitalization during which the increased visibility and mobility of African American writers and travelers, emphasized in Wells's travel essays, become even more pronounced.[8] Indeed, W. E. B. Du Bois, in an open letter to President Warren G. Harding in the March 1921 *Crisis,* underscores this increased mobility with the following appeal: "WE WANT THE RIGHT TO VOTE. WE WANT TO TRAVEL WITHOUT INSULT. WE WANT LYNCHING AND MOB-LAW QUELLED FOREVER. WE WANT FREEDOM FOR OUR BROTHERS IN HAITI."[9] That Du Bois would include the ability to travel without insult in a list including the right to vote and a plea to end lynching and colonial domination points to the connections that black travel writers during this period were making between increased mobility and efforts to expand civil rights and end racial violence. Hurston's Caribbean travel narrative covers similar ideological ground and parallels Wells's essays in its exploration of the relationship between cultural authority and the black female traveler's mobile body. In many travel narratives this relationship challenges the male gaze (what Mary Louise Pratt calls the "imperial eye"),[10] which immobilizes the body of the other while obscuring the white male body housing the objectifying gaze. Framing my book with these two women writers highlights the significant contributions of women to the tradition of African American travel writing and foregrounds the important role that these African American–authored texts themselves play in shaping our understanding of the genre.[11]

The authors under consideration here travel abroad during the beginning and into the height of the Jim Crow era and in the context of the violence and social constraints attending segregationist policy. Wells's antilynching work occurred just before the legalizing of segregation through *Plessy v. Ferguson* in 1896, a decision that emphasized the necessity of her efforts. Hurston's anthropological work in the Caribbean occurred just prior to *Gaines v. Canada* (1938), in which the NAACP's Charles Hamilton Houston convinced the Supreme Court that Missouri (and by extension all states) must either build separate law schools for blacks, equal to those of whites, or integrate graduate schools. *Gaines v. Canada* instigated the rupturing of school segregation laws that would culminate in *Brown v. Board of Education* in 1954. The changing landscape of U.S. civil rights policy during this period created a volatile and complicated context for travel within the United States and influenced writers' reflections on the differing racial climate in other locations outside the country to which they traveled.

While I examine African American travel writing from abroad that is engaged with the material realities of the Jim Crow era, I also stress the particular discursive forms of such texts and the range of cultural work that these travelers undertake, in contrast to the leisure travel agendas of others during this time. As cultural representations, these narratives exhibit what Stephen Greenblatt calls "resonance," the power of objects "to reach out beyond . . . formal boundaries to a larger world, to evoke in the viewer the complex, dynamic cultural forces from which [they have] emerged."[12] In addition to approaching the travel narratives themselves as discursive objects, we might also consider the resonance of the specific physical and discursive objects with which these writers deal in their texts, such as the visual images and photographs that Wells manipulates or the cultural artifacts and practices that Hurston interprets.

Greenblatt's ideas about resonance and cultural boundaries inform my analysis of both the literal and metaphorical movement represented in the African American travel narrative. In terms of their cultural intervention or cultural work, these narratives negotiate cultural boundaries even as they actively establish such boundaries. Greenblatt notes that "if culture functions as a structure of limits, it also functions as the regulator and guarantor of movement. Indeed the limits are virtually meaningless without movement; it is only through improvisation, experiment, and exchange that cultural boundaries can be established." The ratio between mobility and constraint will vary in different cultures, but both are necessary to some degree for cultural survival. Greenblatt further argues that works of art "do not merely passively reflect the prevailing ratio of mobility and constraint;

they help to shape, articulate, and reproduce it through their own improvisatory intelligence" and "variations upon received themes."[13] Heather Russell makes a related claim about African Atlantic narratives, which articulate the "material truths" of their specific contexts "while simultaneously destabilizing Grand Narrative determinism."[14] I argue that the African American travel narrative deals with issues of identity in relation to mobility, cultural displacement, and the "reshaped sense of self,"[15] which we might expect to find in most travel narratives, while also offering significant variations on these common themes. The effort that these narratives exert in pushing against the boundaries governing human mobility and constraint constitutes the cultural work of African American travel narratives from abroad during the Jim Crow era.

I am interested in the types of movements that the African American travel narrative sustains and the cultural limits with which it contends. Despite the fact that Hurston draws attention to the dialectic between movement and stasis during her Caribbean travels, the African American travel narrative typically emphasizes mobility over stasis. The cultural work that the genre undertakes in order to understand and represent African American mobility generates specific discursive spaces for the construction of identity. Wells's and Hurston's travel texts perform similar cultural work in some respects, but their differences remind us that not all African American travelers share the same ideological agendas or enact the same cultural interventions. Indeed, there is a significant heterogeneity generally found in travel literature that can also be found in African American travel literature during this time.[16] The differences between Wells's and Booker T. Washington's travel narratives illustrate this point. Wells's essays document the historical legacy of slavery by way of the lasting material realities of segregation and violence in the United States, while Washington's European travel narrative *The Man Farthest Down* (1912) elides historical realities and concentrates on the notion of class uplift in Europe, especially as it coincides with his agenda of racial uplift at Tuskegee Institute.[17] Wells's travel narratives are published in the form of newspaper essays and as dispatches from a correspondent abroad, while Washington publishes a book of his European travels in collaboration with his white travel companion, the sociologist Robert E. Park. Both Wells and Washington participate in cultural work and explore issues of mobility and identity in African American travel, but they imagine different sets of constraints that define the boundaries of the genre and arrive at different conclusions about the meaning and purposes of African American mobility in the Jim Crow era.

African American travel writing emerges from a rich but troubled narrative of black movement that continues to influence the genre in the late nineteenth and early twentieth centuries. The forced travel of the slave trade[18] and the displacement of African Americans within the United States during northern migration following Reconstruction forge close connections between mobility and African American identity. As Farah Jasmine Griffin argues, both the slave and the migration narrative are associated with images of violence, but the migration narrative specifically invokes the issue of lynching, especially important in the travel writing of Wells, Washington, and Jessie Redmon Fauset. Griffin observes that figures of "hanging bodies, burned and mutilated, women, raped and tormented . . . populate the migration narrative. The texts are filled to the brim with the portrayal of an institutionalized terrorism that daily inflicts itself on the lives of black characters. Lynching becomes a metaphor for all such acts of violence on Southern blacks."[19] Violence, rather than economic or political factors, is the major catalyst for migration in literary texts from the period, according to Griffin, a notion borne out by a March 1920 *Crisis* cartoon that Griffin reproduces in her study of the subject, *"Who Set You Flowin'?" The African-American Migration Narrative* (1995). The cartoon, bearing the caption "The Reason," depicts an African American man, suitcase packed and heading north, looking back over his shoulder at a lynched black body hanging from a tree and a white southerner gesturing toward it. As Griffin demonstrates, the cartoon emphasizes the close connections between lynching and northern migration in the cultural imagination of early twentieth-century African American writers.

Such spectacles of racial violence certainly motivate Wells to travel north and abroad, but the influences of migration in Washington's and Hurston's work might also be viewed in terms of a southern rather than a northern trajectory. As I discuss in chapter 2, a major impetus for Washington's working trip to Europe was to solidify his arguments about African Americans' vocational opportunities in the South. In the case of Hurston, Hazel Carby notes that her immersion in and celebration of black southern life serves as a nostalgic counternarrative to black northern migration and urbanization. Carby argues that Hurston refused to "take seriously" the ways in which northern migration was transforming African American culture and responded to these dramatic transformations by representing African American culture "as primarily rural and oral." Furthermore, Carby claims that the southernness of Hurston's black characters "is not defined through a difference to northernness as much as it is related to cultural practices and beliefs of the Caribbean."[20] In contrast, Eve E. Dunbar contends that Hurston's "black rural modernity" in *Mules and Men* (1935) and *Tell My Horse* carves out a discursive space in which she can combat racism in the United States, though she has to emphasize the primitive nature of non-U.S. blacks in order to do so.[21] Certainly a southerly orientation informs and complicates the meaning of travel and the representation of mobile black bodies in the travel writing of both Hurston and Washington.

My examination of the meaning of black bodies in transit during the age of Jim Crow is also informed by Sidonie Smith's point that "the mode of moving a body through space affects the traveler who moves through space as that body" as well as "the meaning that the traveler sends back home in narration."[22] Differing modes of travel organize black bodies and experience in specific ways, thus influencing the cultural work of these narratives and the discursive space they provide for the exploration of identity. Griffin and Cheryl J. Fish lament the lack of critical attention to such issues in black travel writing when, in their introduction to *A Stranger in the Village: Two Centuries of African-American Travel Writing* (1998), they note that scholars' failure to "account for the significance of mobility" and its relationship to identity in African American travel narratives results from a tendency to read such narratives as autobiography rather than in relation to the unique qualities of travel writing.[23] Important studies of the African diaspora and black Atlantic do not specifically focus on the ways in which the African American travel text influences writers' depictions of the relationship between mobility and identity. Paul Gilroy's volume *The Black Atlantic: Modernity and Double Consciousness* (1993),[24] for example, examines the cultural hybrid of the black Atlantic as an effect of mobility, but he focuses on this cultural hybrid as a source of and catalyst for modernity and not in relation to the genre traits of the black travel narrative. In this book I address this gap in scholarship by examining the ways in which the genre of the African American travel narrative takes up issues of mobility and identity in the late nineteenth and early twentieth centuries and how these travelers and their texts perform cultural work by challenging dominant ideologies about African American experience, expression, and identity in this period of rapid change and racial violence.

African American travel writing presents a particularly under-studied aspect of the genre's history. Travel writing has gained recognition over the past few decades as an important field of study, but as Peter Hulme and Tim Youngs contend, the "complex history" of this "broad and ever-shifting genre . . . has yet to be properly studied."[25] Both Mary Baine Campbell and Alasdair Pettinger note that critical approaches to travel writing must and do change as scholars consider previously under-examined travel texts,[26] a point that Griffin and Fish anticipate when they suggest that the relationship between mobility and identity for African American travelers becomes more clear as African American travel writing receives greater attention.

Postcolonial scholarship has helped us better understand the power dynamics at play in travel texts between mobility and identity. Paul Smethurst contends that European mobility allowed and informed imperial exploration and discourse through the production of a binary privileging the "West's mobility, science and (modern) *progress*" over "the historical and geographical *stasis* of 'the Rest' " of the world. Imperial discourse relies on this system of binaries to suppress the inherent instability and disorder that accompany mobility, giving rise to an imperial form that attempts to order and control "disorderly mobility." Such orderliness is maintained by way of a narrative voice, structure, and other formal elements (such as motifs or images) that impose narrative patterns replicating the "authority of imperial order."[27] A particularly cogent example of this process can be found in the ways that the travel book industry colluded with mapmaking, economic priorities, ethnographic practices, and settlement patterns to effectively colonize the African Congo.[28] Smethurst also notes that the relationship between imperial ideology and the orderly form of imperialist travel writing can break down in various ways: "The main threat to textual orderliness comes from the essential link between travel writing and *mobility*. . . . But if mobility is enabling for the imperialist traveler, it is also potentially threatening and disorderly" because "travel produces the overlapping of conflicting spaces and temporalities of heterotopias, which are the problematised sites where order and form no longer confer meaning on words and things."[29]

Although African American travel texts during the Jim Crow era are not always engaged in deconstructing the imperial forms imposed by the British Empire specifically, these narratives resist hegemonic forces and discourses that threaten to overwhelm or discount black mobilities. Black travel texts participate in the sort of heterotopic exigencies that problematize orderliness. The dichotomy between order and disorder in the travel narrative coincides with what John Zilcosky posits as the "central generic attribute" of travel writing—that is, the inherent tension between truth and fiction, the "built-in anxiety" about the precariousness of its truth claims that distinguishes it from other autobiographical genres.[30] As we consider the tensions in African American travel writing between truth and fiction, between order and disorder, and between the actual movement of black bodies across time and space (in direct challenge to the literal and literary forms of containment forced upon black bodies by dominant cultures) and the literary creation of black selves in the pages of travel accounts, we uncover important characteristics of the African American travel writing produced during this period.

The genre of the travel narrative has always been difficult to define or codify, and some critics, such as Jan Borm, question whether travel writing is a genre at all, viewing the travel book as a hybrid text or "generic *in-betweener*" that complicates attempts to categorize it.[31] Some definitions of travel writing as a genre are so open-ended that almost any text, fictional or factual, dealing with travel, even in a tangential fashion, could be counted as such. Often critics avoid specific definitions altogether by arguing that, like the narratives of mobility it encompasses, the genre itself is fluid and in flux. Alfred Bendixen and Judith Hamera identify two general emphases in travel literature: a focus on the self as "part of an autobiographical project . . . to explain oneself . . . to the reading public" and a "focus on the external details of nature and society in a specific location." Although the first type obviously bleeds into life writing (the title of books such as Sidonie Smith's *Moving Lives* [2001] suggests the overlap between travel writing and autobiography) and the second shares affinities with other forms of discourse such as historical writing, journalism, scientific observation, and sociology, Bendixen and Hamera maintain that travel writing "emerges in unique ways in response to the historical, political, and aesthetic particulars of a given context."[32]

In the past few decades, the establishment of book series, academic journals, scholarly societies, conferences, and a body of critical and theoretical approaches specific to travel writing studies underscores the unique response of travel writing to human mobility. The enduring amorphous nature of travel writing, however, is perhaps anticipated in its critical history. Philip

Gould observes that travel writing in eighteenth-century British America "was not really an identifiable literary genre. Rather, the discourses of travel permeated all sorts of genres and writings that included a wide array of audiences and intentions." This generic openness is illustrated by one of the earliest forms of travel literature, "the promotional writing meant to attract emigrants and funding for British colonies," which was, as Wayne Franklin writes, "less concerned with the details of an actual endured journey than with the general design of America as a scene for potential ones."[33]

The idea of the United States as a tabula rasa designed for potential adventures and onto which the traveler might project his or her desires for a better life does not account for the experience of enslaved Africans, however, as they are brought to the new world. Indeed, African American oral narratives, such as the story of the flying Africans or Ibo Landing, for example, complicate the notion of the promotional tract as the ur-text of American travel writing. The stories shared among African American slaves of field workers who, at the shout of an overseer, rise into the air and fly back to Africa, or of shackled slaves who, upon disembarking from slave ships at the Georgia coastal island port of Ibo Landing, walk back across the water to Africa, depend on the idea of travel back to an African homeland and away from the hostile space of the United States.[34] These stories inform African American mobility and call attention to a sense of identity and mobility that contradicts the narratives of American economics and exceptionalism on which the early promotional tracts depended.

Because of the specific cultural and identity politics informing black travel, the African American travel account often undertakes cultural work more aggressively and with more urgency than narratives by white travelers. This cultural work manifests itself in various ways during the Jim Crow era. As Wells's and Hurston's travel narratives demonstrate, African American travelers often place particular emphasis in their travel writing on the relationship between mobility and corporeality, which Virginia Whatley Smith connects to the slave narrative's account of "shocked bodies and fractured psyches."[35] Furthermore, African American travelers address sociological context in ways that often aggressively rework the leisure-class tourist narrative, as Wells, Washington, and Fauset demonstrate. In terms of national identity, Bendixen and Hamera insist that for all American travelers, "American self-assertion is more vigorous on foreign soil." While this is true for some of the travelers I examine, the notion of individual or national self-assertion itself is often challenged by the African American travelers discussed here. Bendixen and Hamera seem to elide race and even gender when they suggest that "the traveler's persona stands in for Americanness" when Americans are abroad and then list some of the personae that Americans adopt: the expat, the tourist, the good-natured American gentleman, the sailor who "goes native," and the adventurer.[36] These are positions that assume a certain amount of white male privilege, and the African American travelers whom I discuss often adopt an ironic or critical attitude toward or actively work to distance themselves from such identities.

African American travelers also express reasons for traveling that may differ from those of white travelers. For example, cultural critique and observation often trump leisure as a motivation for African American travel. Bendixen and Hamera note that whereas a "privileged Euro-American traveler might construct travel to Europe or the Middle East in terms of various 'origin myths,' as return visits to lands that are part of one's historical or cultural ancestry, African American travelers pointedly problematize these myths by naming complicity with slavery and white amnesic nostalgia as their core, if unacknowledged, components."[37] Thus Wells explicitly rejects the tourist sites and institutions of London (the British Museum, the Royal Academy, or Westminster Abbey, for example) that might be complicit with cultural or racial oppression and characterizes herself as too busily engaged in her antiracism work to act the part of tourist or pilgrim.[38] She deemphasizes these roles in order to promote the important antilynching message of her lecture tour and establish herself as a credible eyewitness to racial violence. Wells claims cultural and narrative authority by downplaying the conventional focus on the traveler's gaze in the genre of the travel narrative and drawing attention to her mobile black body.

Hurston even more explicitly comments on the charged racial atmosphere in Jamaica, which invokes some of the physical realities of Reconstruction-era American racism, such as segregation and lynching. She notes that the privileging of whiteness in Jamaica is "a curious spectacle to the eyes of an American Negro" and says she feels as if she has "stepped back to the days of slavery or the generation immediately after surrender" in the United States.[39] Hurston's discussion of racial prejudice and black female oppression underscores how the violence against the black female population in Jamaica parallels racial wrongs in the United States. African American travelers' critical views of their own or others' mobility in the context of segregation emphasize the unique and disruptive nature of black movement, particularly as it relates to issues of self and cultural identity and authority in travel texts written during the age of Jim Crow.

In addition to works by Wells and Hurston, I examine other texts from this period that grapple with African American mobility, identity, and cultural authority, including Washington's *The Man Farthest Down* (1912), Matthew Henson's *A Negro Explorer at the North Pole* (1912), and Fauset's 1921 and 1925–26 travel essays published in *Crisis* magazine. I explore African American travel writing that has not yet been studied extensively (Henson and Fauset) or that has been studied as a sociological or anthropological treatise but not as travel writing (Wells, Washington, and Hurston). In chapter 1 I analyze Wells's body as physical proof of the potentially empowering aspects of mobility and show how Wells herself serves as an example of the ways in which the African American community might resist historical narratives of inequality and achieve cultural power. In chapter 2 I contrast Washington's approach with that of Wells. The close ties in Washington's travel account between the traveler's physical mobility and the race's upward social mobility leads to an elision of racial history and a representation of mobility and constraint that is very different from Wells's bold critique of segregation. Washington's travels and narrative reveal the power of racial ideologies and the ways in which they complicate the traveler's identity and agenda. Similar to Wells, Washington attempts in his narrative to reimagine African American mobility and the genre of the African American travel text in liberating ways (most obviously by pitting his text against the conventional slave narrative), but his problematic position on issues such as lynching and the black business class, as well as his desire to validate his views of work and progress embodied by Tuskegee Institute, cause him to sustain Old South ideals in his travel text.

Similar tendencies appear in Washington's brief introduction to *A Negro Explorer at the North Pole* (1912), an account of Matthew Henson's 1909 North Pole expedition with Robert Peary. Washington downplays Henson's role in the discovery of the pole and notes his "useful[ness]," "fidelity," and "devotion" to Peary.[40] Peary also supplies a foreword to the narrative, characterizing Henson as a credit to his race. In my examination of Henson's travel narrative in chapter 3, I observe how this framing of an African American text recalls the rhetoric and design of slave narrative prefaces, usually written by white men to legitimize the text. In his text, however, Henson resists the confining cultural, structural, and linguistic forces of the slave narrative form and incorporates genre traits of the European exploration narrative. The tension in the text between the genres of the exploration and slave narrative challenge Eurocentric notions about both the subjects and the work of exploration and discovery; such a challenge represents an important aspect of the cultural work that the African American travel text performs during the Jim Crow period. Henson's text pushes against the constraints of these narrative traditions, and he claims authority as a traveler as he explores what happens when a black body occupies the position generally reserved for the white explorer.

In chapter 4 I examine Jessie Redmon Fauset's less explicit claims to the African American traveler's authority in her *Crisis* travel essays from 1921 and 1925–26, in which she sets the everyday realities of her life abroad against scenes of poverty and oppression. Writing of France, for example, she eloquently describes the lack of heating in her *pension* and the lengths to which landlords will go to avoid providing it. Such commentary contrasts dramatically with the conditions of the poor on which she reflects in her essays "Dark Algiers the White" and "This Way to the Flea Market." Fauset's observation in "Yarrow Revisited" that in France she can take her meals in whatever tearoom "*takes [her] fancy*,"[41] alluding to the lack of such freedom in Jim Crow America and emphasizing her increased mobility in Europe, provides a stark contrast with her discussion of class oppression (a topic also appearing in the travel texts of both Washington and Wells) and reveals how the mundane experiences of travel abroad and their formal depiction in African American travel writing from this period highlight issues of cultural power, identity, and mobility.

Fauset was often regarded as part of the Harlem Renaissance's "Rear Guard," the conventional, "imitative" writers who avoided innovative form and content in order to court white critical approval, and her work has been criticized as "sentimental" and "dull."[42] Yet readers' undue concerns about the perceived middle-class sensibilities of Fauset's *Crisis* essays, including her travel pieces, eclipse the more radical impulses of this writing. Indeed, we might consider the combination of conservatism and activism in Fauset's essays a reflection of the "discourse of respectability" that Evelyn Brooks Higginbotham identifies in the Black Baptist Church Women's Movement of the late nineteenth and early twentieth centuries. Higginbotham notes that Baptist women during this period "emphasized manners and morals while simultaneously asserting traditional forms of protest, such as petitions, boycotts, and verbal appeals to justice."[43] Given the challenge posed by the movement to representations of black women as either mammies or Jezebels, we could also view Wells's emphasis on respectability and her efforts to resist negative characterizations of the black female body within this same context. And although Fauset's essays may at first blush seem disengaged from important racial issues, a more careful reading reveals that this is not the case; indeed, the fact that we find her essays published alongside reports of lynchings in *The Crisis* (for example, her article "Sunday Afternoon" appears just before the NAACP's report on U.S. lynchings from 1885 to 1922 in the February 1922 issue) underscores parallels between the contexts of racial violence informing Fauset's and Wells's travel writing.[44] Furthermore, the tension between conservative and radical impulses in Fauset's work, what we might view as a passive versus an active stance toward cultural issues, invokes the tension between order and disorder that Smethurst describes, as well as the dialectic between stasis and mobility that Greenblatt identifies as a feature of the cultural work that texts perform and which Hurston explicitly notes of her travels in the Caribbean.

In addition to exploring this dialectic in her travels, Hurston, similarly to Henson, claims cultural and narrative authority by occupying a position often designated as the province of white men. Hurston's use of the participant observer persona raises the question of what it means when an African American woman fills this role often occupied by a white male researcher. Scholars have characterized Hurston's unique approach as "improvising ethnography" or a function of her "erratic temperament."[45] In chapter 5 I consider her innovative style as a function of her physical mobility and examine her text in relation to the genre traits of the travel text. Through the liberated mobility and cultural work of her Caribbean travels, Hurston reimagines slavery's Middle Passages as routes that mobilize and authorize black female bodies to participate in the preservation of stories and culture and the literal and metaphorical transmission of bodies of knowledge across oceans.

Through an examination of the relationship between mobility and identity in African American travel texts during a period of cultural change, this book provides insights into the way late nineteenth- and early twentieth-century African American travel narratives challenge dominant ideologies about African American experience and history. The differing stances taken in these texts toward issues of mobility and identity also reveal the variability of the African American travel text. Indeed, I have chosen the writers and texts under consideration because of this variability, but also because through such variation they demonstrate shared patterns and themes. As I demonstrate, African American travel writers during the Jim Crow era perform cultural work in several ways: literally, through their cultural interventions abroad; aesthetically, through their negotiation of the tensions that characterize travel writing as a genre; and rhetorically, through their arguments about the complex relationship between mobility and identity in African American travel.

1

EMBODYING SEGREGATION

Ida B. Wells on the Antilynching Circuit

Writing about the return voyage from her first trip to the United Kingdom in 1893, Ida B. Wells notes two "delightful" circumstances of the journey: "First, there were few if any white Americans on board. Second, there were fifteen young Englishmen in one party . . . [who] were as courteous and attentive to me as if my skin had been of the fairest." She identifies this voyage as the first time that white people had extended to her "the courtesy they would have offered to any lady of their own race," emphasizing the racially segregated nature of her environment and experience up to this point. Yet her shipboard narrative does not utterly surmount the logic of segregation, since she also reports that the Englishmen "seemed to take great pleasure in shocking onlookers by their courteous and respectful attention" to her.[1]

Indeed, as Alasdair Pettinger reveals, the racial policies of transatlantic steamers were far from settled during the period. Some black ocean travelers tended to represent experiences of segregation aboard ship "as simply signs of the intermediary character of the transatlantic voyage, a compound of (good) British and (bad) American ways of doing things, so that any unpleasantness might be seen as merely the residue of what has been left behind (if traveling east) or an anticipation of what is to come (if traveling west)." Pettinger argues, however, that the ocean becomes a more fluid space and "the discrimination faced by passengers cannot be deduced from . . . more settled policies in force on either side of the ocean."[2] Wells reveals that the courtesy she experiences onboard depends on such an ambivalently racialized and hostile context for its effect. The young men's treatment of her emphasizes Wells's position as exotic Other, the highly visible and racially marked object of the young men's spectacle of civility.

During her antilynching tours in the United Kingdom in 1893 and 1894, Wells draws on the general tropes of travel and the specific relationship between mobility and subjectivity in black experience to critique U.S. segregation and its attendant violence. This critique appears in the autobiographical account of her 1893 tour and in her column "Ida B. Wells Abroad," published in the *Chicago Inter-Ocean,* detailing her 1894 tour. Although the title of her column emphasizes her position as traveler, Wells resists tourist spectacle in both the column and her autobiography in order to promote the cultural work of her travels and establish herself as a credible and embodied eyewitness to segregation and lynching. Ultimately, the act of traveling as a form of cultural work (rather than tourist pleasure) functions as a trope for the ways in which the African American community might resist historical narratives of segregation and inequality and move toward greater cultural power. In her transatlantic writing, speaking, and traveling, Wells's mobile black body becomes corporeal proof of the potentially empowering aspects of physical and cultural mobility.

In the preface to her autobiography, Wells notes that she writes her life story for young black readers who know "little of our race's history" beyond the Civil War, so that they might understand "how the agitation against the lynching evil began."[3] The important work of Wells's antilynching campaign is well illustrated by her published pamphlets before (*Southern Horrors: Lynch Law in All Its Phases* [1892]) and after (*A Red Record: Tabulated Statistics and Alleged Causes of Lynchings in the United States, 1892–1893–1894* [1895]) her trips to the United Kingdom. Wells's autobiography and column from abroad also focus on the difficulty of achieving equality and exposing the horrors of lynching. While the tropes of travel and tourism are evident in her column, most likely appealing to readers eager for dispatches from a special correspondent abroad, the column functions chiefly as a polemic against lynching. By positioning her writing and traveling persona against familiar tropes of leisure travel, Wells rejects not only the role of tourist but also the various images of the black traveler constructed in other key texts, such as those by Olaudah Equiano, Mary Seacole, Frederick Douglass, A. B. C. Merriman-Labor, and Matthew Henson. Equiano's (1789) and Seacole's (1857) picaresque narratives frequently emphasize the adventure and fantastic sights of travel, while Douglass characterizes himself as a tourist at a Robert Burns monument in Scotland in 1846 and at Egyptian historical sites and museums in his unpublished travel diary of 1886–87. Merriman-Labor in *Britons through,* while Henson, as I discuss in chapter 3, emphasizes the adventure and imperial contexts of exploration in *A Negro Explorer at the North Pole* (1912).[4]

Wells distances her travels from the romantic sights and adventures emphasized in many of these writings. Indeed, when the *Memphis Daily Commercial* suggested that she was simply a "Negro Adventuress" and vilified her work, she responded in her *Inter-Ocean* dispatch of May 28, 1894, that if the same effort to "conceal the facts were exercised to put a stop to lynching," she would not need to rehearse such atrocities.[5] By dissociating her travels from romance and spectacle and insisting on the truth of the barbaric lynching incidents she describes, Wells also defines her work and travel against the fantastic, which, as Hélène Christol argues, often becomes "a crucial literary mode" in the context of the black Atlantic.[6] Wells's rejection of both the touristic and the fantastic produces what Paul Gilroy terms the black Atlantic's "redemptive critique" of modernity and history.[7] Retracing the historical transatlantic routes of the Middle Passage, Wells's travel alludes, in the words of Peter Linebaugh and Marcus Rediker, to the "transformed . . . experience of work" that resulted as trading routes were established and peoples throughout the Atlantic world were forced into slavery and servitude.[8] But unlike Africans traveling the original Middle Passages, "literally suspended in the 'oceanic' " dimensions or "*nowhere*" of the Atlantic's "undifferentiated identity," to borrow Hortense J. Spillers's terms,[9] Wells challenges notions of enforced travel, slave labor, and diminished subjectivity through the liberated mobility, definitive agenda, and cultural work of her trips abroad. In doing so, she reimagines slavery's transatlantic passages as routes that mobilize black bodies to resist segregation and violence and move toward empowerment.

In her first *Inter-Ocean* dispatch, published April 2, 1894, Wells draws connections between her travels abroad and the oppressive racial atmosphere of the United States. Following the "suppression" of her Memphis newspaper, *Free Speech,* in May 1892, she was unable to generate American concern for her antilynching efforts, but she discovered sympathetic audiences in the United Kingdom in 1893 who paved the way for her second tour in 1894. She admits the strangeness of going abroad when, logically, more good might come of such a campaign in the United States, save that "we, as a race, cannot get a hearing in the United States," where both "the press and pulpit" are silent about, and thus complicit in, lynch law. She hopes that the example of the English press and clergy in denouncing lynching will produce a similar response in the United States.[10] Wells's need to cross national borders to accomplish her aims illustrates Gilroy's point that the "modern political and cultural formation" of the black Atlantic derives its specificity "through [a] desire to transcend both the structures of the nation state and the constraints of ethnicity and national particularity."[11] Wells exhibits the desire to escape such limitations when she characterizes her experience in Europe as a rebirth,[12] language that indicates, as Gilroy suggests, the transformative nature of transnational experience.[13] Unlike many African Americans abroad, who, as Carolyn Karcher reminds us, either settled permanently in Europe or embraced pan-Africanism, Wells, though she eventually returned to the United States, underwent "an alteration of consciousness akin to both a religious conversion and a change of nationality" and argued for the right of individual African Americans to emigrate to Africa or remain in America, a position typifying, according to Karcher, "the transnationalism of the Black Atlantic."[14]

Wells's article of April 9, 1894, from Liverpool, reveals her developing transnational consciousness and its role in her antilynching campaign. She reminds readers that Liverpool was the English center of "slave interests" from the Elizabethan period to the British abolition of slavery in 1807 and that the majority of the slave ships traversing the black Atlantic "were built in the Liverpool docks and owned by Liverpool merchants." Despite Liverpool's investment in the slave trade, however, she notes that the city "has learned that [it] can prosper without the slave trade or slave labor." Liverpool's complex slave history provides a dramatic backdrop for the distinctions that Wells draws between the segregated United States and a progressive Liverpool, where a "colored person" can ride in public transportation without insult, stay in hotels and eat in restaurants without incident, and freely move about in art galleries and churches. "It is like being born into another world," she writes, "to be welcomed among persons of the highest order of intellectual and social culture as if . . . one of themselves." As further proof of her increased physical and cultural mobility, she notes that in the course of two weeks she has, by invitation, delivered ten speeches refuting the idea "that Negro men are despoilers . . . of white women." She juxtaposes the cultural message of her travels with the slander of white American transatlantic travelers who "draw a picture of the isolated district in the South where great hordes of ignorant and dangerous Negroes swarm; of the inadequacy and delay of the law; and then ask, 'What would you do if your wife or daughter were so assaulted?' "[15] Wells counters the assumptions about African Americans supported by such rhetoric through her frequent references to the mobility and respect that she enjoys in the United Kingdom.

Wells again emphasizes her increased mobility and the urgency of her cultural work abroad in her article of May 19, 1894, in which she declares that she has "been so constantly traveling and speaking" that she has been unable to write. Her unrelenting schedule also prevents her from sightseeing. She contrasts her travel agenda with that of the tourist, acknowledging the attractions awaiting the tourist in the United Kingdom but representing herself as a committed advocate for justice who rejects the temptation to sightsee rather than work. In an earlier article of April 23, 1894, Wells describes potential tourist attractions, including Manchester's shipping port, its great canal to be opened by Queen Victoria in June, the "public buildings . . . black with the centuries of smoke and dust," and the convenient layout of its art galleries, but then devotes the majority of the article to the antilynching theme. Similarly, in her article of June 25, 1894, Wells opens with travel guide–like observations, mimicking tourists' complaints about the weather or cramped railway compartments, but these details of tourist culture become the vehicle through which she critiques U.S. segregation, noting that "primitive as are these railway carriages, I as a Negro can ride in them free from insult or discrimination on account of color, and that's what I cannot do in many States of my own free (?) America." Further invoking tourist tropes, she notes that the "charm of antiquity and historic association" is evident throughout London, including the home of her host, P. W. Clayden (editor of the *London Daily News*), across the street from Dickens's London residence and only a few minutes' walk from the British Museum. But she writes that she is "too engrossed in the work which brought [her] here" to act the tourist at the British Museum, the Royal Academy, or Westminster Abbey.[16]

Wells's depiction of travel as cultural work anticipates Booker T. Washington's transatlantic travels two decades later, recorded in *The Man Farthest Down* (1912), which he similarly characterizes as work rather than pleasure, as I discuss in chapter 2. He travels to Europe to gauge the conditions of southern blacks in relation to those of the European laborer, a comparison that allows him to promote industrial education. In order to better experience working conditions in Europe, he believes that he must "leave the ordinary beaten track of European travel" and experience "the grime and dirt of everyday life" among Europe's laboring poor.[17] Unlike Wells, however, Washington seems willing to ignore historical slavery and contemporary segregation in order to promote industrial education, and is even somewhat acquiescent on the subject of lynching. Furthermore, in *The Man Farthest Down,* he sometimes characterizes slave history as a series of romanticized adventure stories, thus distancing himself from the historical specificity and material reality of slavery and its legacy of segregation and violence.

In contrast, Wells's notion of cultural work does not ignore the historical legacy of slavery and the lasting conditions of segregation and violence in the United States; rather, her articles and lectures are steeped in them. Not only does she share specific examples of lynchings with her British audiences (and at one breakfast meeting passes around an image of the lynching of C. J. Miller), but also she connects her work and trip to the historical work of other black leaders and the narrative of black struggle against segregation.[18] In her autobiography, Wells registers the important differences between her approach and that of Washington, differences that are informed by their fundamentally different attitudes toward segregation in the United States.

Her acquaintance with Washington began when she wrote to him on November 30, 1890, praising his "manly criticism of our corrupt and ignorant ministry."[19] Her admiring letter masks her nuanced opinion of Washington, however, for she was displeased that he would choose Boston as the city from which to voice complaints against the moral and intellectual inferiority of the southern black clergy, and she wrote an editorial in *Free Speech* criticizing him.[20] Her 1890 letter to Washington implies her displeasure: "I have long since seen that some one of the name & standing of yourself, *among ourselves,* must call a halt and be the Martin Luther of our times in condemning the practices of our ministers."[21] Her emphasis of the phrase "among ourselves" suggests that this critique must be performed by someone from within the black community, but it also implies that such critique should be kept within the black community. Indeed, she notes in the autobiography that while there might be truth in Washington's statement, "it was a wrong thing for him to have made that criticism in a white paper so far away from home [in the North]. When the people needed such criticism, I felt he ought to have done as we did—tell them about it at home rather than tell our enemies abroad."[22]

Later, Wells would become an outspoken critic of Washington, particularly of his unwillingness to oppose lynching more firmly, and she was consistently critical of his accommodationist stand on segregation, which she saw as ultimately fostering attitudes and stereotypes leading to violence against African Americans. According to Wells, Washington refused to ally himself with her and the Afro-American Council because of their radical politics and seemed more interested in promoting his theory that blacks "had better give attention to trying to be first-class people in a jim crow car than insisting that the jim crow car should be abolished."[23] As Patricia Schechter observes, Wells was also critical of Washington's characterization of blacks in his speeches and jokes and "blamed [him] personally for circulating negative stereotypes of black people to whites—especially those of the chicken thief and the layabout, uneducated 'darky' preacher," stereotypes that supported "assumptions about black criminality and moral deviance and traveled all too quickly to a supposed inclination to rape."[24] Years after Wells's trips abroad, when Julius Rosenwald (president of Sears Roebuck and a Tuskegee supporter) regaled Wells and the NAACP with an account of Washington's "chicken-stealing stories" delivered at a Standard Club meeting, Wells rejoined, "A great many of us cannot approve Mr. Washington's plan of telling chicken-stealing stories on his own people in order to amuse his audiences and get money for Tuskegee."[25] In perhaps her most succinct criticism of Washington's position, Wells exposes the direct relationship between Jim Crow and lynch law: "Mr. Washington knows . . . that lynching is not invoked to punish crime but color, and not even industrial education will change that."[26] Unlike Washington, who Wells sees as willing to voice criticisms of his own people "abroad" in the North, Wells journeys overseas to spread her antilynching message among international allies rather than among enemies within her "own free (?) America," where she cannot even ride a railway car "free from insult or discrimination on account of color."

Her columns and autobiography are replete with such references to the physical realities of her experiences of segregation, which she uses to lend authority to her antilynching campaign abroad. The corporeal ramifications of her work and travel—their physicality in contrast to the disembodiment of the traveler's gaze—are apparent in the autobiographical account of her first trip to England in 1893, in which Wells reprints an article from the British women's magazine *Ladies Pictorial.* The article describes how she was "dragged out of a railway car in Tennessee and on refusing to go in to the 'Jim Crow car,' was left behind in the station, to the great delight of the passengers who stood up on their seats and applauded the action of the conductor, baggagemaster, and station-master in expelling her." The article suggests the legitimizing function and emotional appeal that Wells's first-hand experiences with segregation could have on audiences, editorializing, "Any one who has traveled through America knows the horrors of the 'colored car,' and will sympathise with Miss Wells." Furthermore, in contrast to Washington's contention that racial uplift is a natural result of African Americans' hard work and conciliation, Wells's experience reveals "that as the Negro advances in education and in the qualities of good citizenship, the disinclination to allow him civil rights becomes deeper." This validation of Wells's experience and message lends authority to her lynching accounts, her "appeals for a fair trial and legal punishment,"[27] and her insistence that black education and progress alone will not counter deeply entrenched segregation and the violence it generates.

Wells's exile from Memphis in 1892 also grants her authority as a witness to the violence generated by segregation. While traveling in the North, she received word that "a committee of leading citizens" had destroyed the offices and type of the *Free Speech* newspaper in Memphis (which she partly owned), threatening death to anyone who revived it. The destruction of the newspaper occurred in retaliation for a May 1892 editorial in which Wells had dared to challenge the "thread-bare lie that Negro men assault white women," warning, "If Southern white men are not careful, they will over-reach themselves and a conclusion will be reached which will be very damaging to the moral reputation of their women."[28] She expressed similar ideas in *Southern Horrors,* her antilynching pamphlet of the same year, in which she characterized black men as "Afro-American Sampsons [*sic*] who suffer themselves to be betrayed by white Delilahs."[29] The retaliation for the editorial was swift, and upon learning that her home was under surveillance by lynchers "who promised to kill [her] on sight," she took a position at the *New York Age* and continued her antilynching work in the North. "They had made me an exile and threatened my life for hinting at the truth," she wrote, declaring that she "owed it" to herself and the race "to tell the whole truth" once in New York, where she "could do so freely." Wells argued that lynching was not motivated by black men raping white women but by black economic success. (Her controversial editorial was inspired by the lynching of three black businessmen who were threatening white business interests.) Lynching was a way to "keep the nigger down," the vehicle to sustain inequality and "stifle Negro manhood" when segregation and other forms of social and political injustice became less efficient.[30]

Wells alludes to these incidents from her own experience throughout her *Inter-Ocean* dispatches, linking her work in England to her earlier antiracism work in the United States and extending to her transatlantic trip the image that she had constructed of herself as an exile within her own country with nothing to lose for telling the whole truth about lynching. In Liverpool, "truth compelled [her] to say that lynching is spreading in the states," though it "grieved" her to do it. In Manchester, writing about her criticism of Frances Willard and others, Wells insists that she seeks only "to tell here what truth has compelled me to say as to the words and actions of some of our American Christians and temperance workers, when asked by British friends to do so." In Bristol, when discussing the refusal of southern churches to admit African Americans, Wells was "asked if Northern churches knew of this discrimination and continued fellowship with the churches which practiced it." She writes, "Truth compelled me to reply in the affirmative," and to describe the prejudice that northern churches practiced in an attempt to court "the good will of the South."[31] Wells's statements emphasize the kind of work and the amount of truth-telling necessary to challenge segregation and lynch law.

If, however, as Gail Bederman observes, lynching was for northerners in the United States largely "an imaginary scenario, constructed and fed by depictions in newspapers and literature," then this was certainly the case for the British as well.[32] Wells works against the assumptions of these imaginings on both sides of the Atlantic to argue for her own authenticity as an eyewitness to such events, adopting a trope that is readily apparent in most travel narratives: that of the seeing eye. Early in her autobiography, she remarks that journalism afforded "an outlet through which to express the real 'me,'" and in the *Inter-Ocean* column she works to convey the sense that readers are getting not only her real self but also the real story. Excerpts that she inserts in her column from newspaper and magazine articles in which other journalists note her unimpassioned voice and the absence of rhetoric in her speeches further establish her objectivity as a traveling eyewitness.[33]

Yet Wells's authority as eyewitness to segregation's horrors chiefly depends on the embodiment of her seeing eye within a black female body that has been marked and despised through segregation and threatened with death by the lynch mob. Her public visibility as an antilynching proponent counters the many ways in which, as Schechter notes, "black women were totally invisible in the dominant lynching story." Schechter observes that Wells began this unmasking of black women in *Southern Horrors,* where she "made black women visible in the dynamics of southern lynching and sexualized racism" as victims of lynching and rape, "assert[ing] black women's claim to outraged womanhood traditionally reserved only for white women." According to Schechter, *Southern Horrors* explicitly "connect[s] the 'private' crime of rape to the 'public' crime of lynching," making visible the violence against black women.[34] Even while exposing the abuse of black bodies, however, Wells retains a desire to "shield the bodies of African Americans, especially women," from "complete exposure" that might perpetuate racist stereotypes or cause humiliation,[35] for example, of the kind resulting from some of Washington's discourse. Not only does Wells draw attention to black women's complex relationship to the lynching issue, but also, as Nicole King has written, she expands "the definition of lynching 'victims' to include not only those hanging in the trees but the entire black community—the collective public body that lynching was meant to terrorize through the example of the particular, dead, victim."[36]

I want to extend this idea further to suggest that Wells's own mobile and public body also acts as a material sign to her British audiences of the collective black body targeted by lynchers. Indeed, as I have implied, Wells's tour, her speeches, and even her demeanor can be viewed as performative.[37] In her biography of Wells, Linda McMurry notes that Wells maintained an interest in public performance and the stage, having "toyed with the idea of becoming an actress,"[38] suggesting the ease and pleasure with which she might have taken up the lecture circuit. The disturbingly public and "masculine" aspects of her lecturing performances were problematic, however, for the way they blurred distinctions between notions of men's and women's work.[39] As Bederman points out, to lecture on issues related to sexuality (such as rape) was hardly proper feminine behavior for a young, unmarried woman; Wells often quoted graphic descriptions of lynchings from southern U.S. newspapers,[40] avoiding direct mention of the unseemly details in her own words.

She also presented herself as a paragon of virtue and womanly attributes to counter rumors about her unsavory past. According to Schechter, white racists and newspapers labeled her "a 'black harlot' in search of a 'white husband,' . . . 'a prostitute bent on miscegenation,' . . . [and] a 'slanderous and nasty-minded mulatress.'"[41] In her autobiography and elsewhere Wells insisted on her virtue, demanding a public apology from a minister who had accused her of unseemly behavior, explaining that she "wanted him to know" that she was a black woman "who had tried to keep herself spotless and morally clean."[42] In a diary entry of June 12, 1886, Wells described two exemplary models of womanhood, which she further developed in her portrait of proper black womanhood titled "The Model Woman: A Pen Picture of the Typical Southern Girl," published in the *New York Freeman* on February 18, 1888, and offered as a "pattern" for young black women.[43] Yet Wells also worried about appearing too feminine; she was concerned over the effect on her audience of her tears during a New York speech in which she described her exile from Memphis and her resulting loneliness and homesickness. (She used similar language to detail these experiences in the chapter of her autobiography titled "The Homesick Exile.") Though Wells excised demonstrations of sentimental weakness from subsequent public appearances, King suggests that she was caught in "the paradoxes of being a Victorian feminist activist"; that "in order to convey the 'truth' Wells was required to perform according to a conventional 'role,'" and her performance of womanly sentiment often worked in her favor.[44] Indeed, Wells sometimes underscores her conventionality even while exposing the absurdity of segregation, emphasizing, for example, in her description of the young white Englishmen's courtesies on her return voyage in 1893, how their attentions confirm that they recognize her as a "lady."[45]

Wells links her performances of respectability and womanliness to her experience of segregation in order to reveal the irrationality of lynch law. She lifts up the lynched black body as evidence against lynching even as she offers her own body as the embodiment of (and an argument against) segregated experience in the United States.[46] One example of this embodiment appears in her antilynching pamphlets, which often displayed Wells's name and an image of her face on the cover, raising important "questions about power and identity," as Schechter suggests, and, in the case of *Southern*

Horrors, "qualif[ying] the effect" of Frederick Douglass's "authenticating" letter of introduction.[47] Theorizing the importance of embodiment in travel texts, Marguerite Helmers and Tilar Mazzeo note that "historically, the implied presence of the body has been one of the ways in which travel writers guarantee the authenticity of their accounts. As a matter of convention, travel writers have assured their readers that their representations have a source in 'first-hand' or 'eye-witness' experience." Furthermore, "as a matter of narrative posturing, the travel account insists that someone actually went somewhere." Wells's narrative posturing as an eyewitness to segregation and lynching, then, not only involves her having been somewhere in terms of travel but also emphasizes that she has "been there" as a black woman experiencing racial discrimination and threats of violence. Helmers and Mazzeo further contend that "while the textual and imaginary body is never contiguous with the 'real' body of a writer, the conventions of the genre promise that its representations have their origins in the materiality of both the subject and the object."[48] In Wells's case, an even more direct link exists between the textual and the actual body of the writer, as well as between the lynched bodies she describes in her column (often vicariously through newspaper accounts) and the images of actual bodies (such as C. J. Miller's) that she presents to her audiences.

Wells's use of real, textual, and photographed bodies invokes tensions between the body and the gaze. Theorists of the gaze have suggested that the scopic desire leads to the erasure of the seeing body in order to focus on the gaze itself, which becomes an ideological apparatus of empire, according to Mary Louise Pratt, and is assumed to originate in a colonizing white male body.[49] As indicated by the scene I described at the beginning of this chapter, with Wells as a black female spectacle on board the ship, Wells's black body is the object of the white male gaze, but that body *also* embodies a countergaze that registers the reactions of others to its disruptive presence. Radhika Mohanram suggests that the erasure of the corporeal in colonial texts acts as a sign of imperial power and access to knowledge of the object,[50] a process well illustrated by Edward Said's theory of Orientalism.[51] But scholars such as Lila Harper and Sara Mills remind us that the erasure of the body is more complicated for women writers or writers of color, whose actual bodies can be read as signs of difference.[52] Women travelers, including women travelers of color, are both seeing and seen, positions that, as Helmers and Mazzeo contend, "the speaking subject constantly negotiates."[53] Thus, while Wells, as a black woman traveler, gazes back, she also finds herself interpellated, to borrow Louis Althusser's term, simultaneously "hailed" as subject by dominant American and European culture, functioning as both eyewitness and embodied racial spectacle. That is, she is a racial body, a segregated body, and even, as her experiences in Memphis show, a potentially lynched body.

We might ask how, in this play of presence and absence, Wells negotiates the erasure of the body that characterizes travel writing as a genre. Sometimes she seems to resist her position as spectacle (as her positive representation of her shipboard experience with the young Englishmen reveals) and distances her writing and experience from the spectacular and fantastic elements of other black travel writing through the emphasis on her cultural work and firsthand eyewitness critique of segregation and lynching. In these instances she appears to deflect attention away from her body to concentrate on the results of her transatlantic travel and labor or the objects of her critical gaze. But on occasion her function as an embodied racial spectacle (toward which the placement of her image on the cover of her pamphlets seems to gesture) erupts through the carefully orchestrated rhetoric of her texts. Her experience as a shipboard spectacle for the young Englishmen is one example. Another occurs at the end of her May 19, 1894, *Inter-Ocean* article, in which she describes meeting Lady Jeune, wife of an eminent British jurist, who assures Wells of a London audience with her friends, "for she thinks they ought to know that the Negro race is not the degraded one she had been led to believe." Lady Jeune wanted Wells to persuade her friends that African Americans are not a "race of rapists,"[54] but the event can also be read as a chance for Wells to demonstrate, through her own body, bearing, and intelligence, that African Americans are not degraded; she is corporeal proof, in this case, against degradation.

Wells's position as a spectacle, and the ways in which she turns such moments to her advantage, is further emphasized by her discussion of Frederick Douglass's appearance at the Chicago World's Fair. African Americans had been denied representation at the fair (Wells had participated in the publication of a pamphlet distributed at the fair denouncing this exclusion), but Douglass was allowed to participate as a representative of Haiti.[55] In her *Inter-Ocean* article of May 28, 1894, Wells notes that the British assume "that such a man [as Douglass], a product of American civilization, was a more wonderful tribute to America's greatness than all the material exhibits stored in the white city." While such a statement turns Douglass into a visible product of American civilization, Wells also signifies on Douglass's objectification as the most important "exhibit" in the "white city" of America when she notes that "the Negro hopes that some day the United States will become as great intellectually and morally as she is *materially*."[56] Since Douglass is the material manifestation of American greatness, this phrase could also be read as a hope that the United States "will become as great intellectually and morally" as Frederick Douglass and African American culture. Douglass (and by extension all African Americans) becomes the truly fine American *material* in this case.

Such ideas coincide with Farah J. Griffin and Cheryl J. Fish's suggestion that the complexities of black subjectivity are often revealed in black travel writing,[57] in this case through Wells's material exhibitions of both respectability and racial injustice. Through these exhibitions, Wells typifies the black Atlantic's "insider-outsider duality" of consciousness,[58] what W. E. B. Du Bois would refer to as "double-consciousness."[59] Karcher argues, perhaps obviously, that this duality is most apparent in Wells's position between two worlds, Britain and America, and in her negotiation of these respective audiences, sometimes representing herself "as an outsider forced into exile by her native land and pleading with strangers for acceptance, sometimes as an insider welcomed as a guest of honor in circles from which her white compatriots would have banned her," and sometimes identifying herself as an American, "conjur[ing] up for her American audience the picture of a world without Jim Crow."[60] Wells's negotiation of these various positions is apparent in her autobiography, where, as Schechter notes, Wells reveals how her British audiences "keyed skin color to [her] credibility."[61] Her hostess, Mrs. Clayden, noted that Wells might have achieved greater success abroad if she "had been a few shades blacker," when only a few pages earlier Wells had expressed her relief at being among people who judge a person on more than "the color of the skin."[62] Schechter reminds us that southern racists "questioned Wells's authority *through* her body," drawing attention to her mixed-race status as white, African American, and American Indian and suggesting that her perspective might thus be "tainted," a charge that she also encountered in London, and to which she replied, "If I have any taint to be ashamed of in myself, it is the taint of *white* blood!"[63] From this perspective, we see Wells involved in a complex performance of transatlantic identity as a woman, a traveler, and an African American of mixed blood.

Nevertheless, Wells's embodied performances of identity are not simply demonstrations of transatlantic double consciousness. Her corporeal fabrications of identity operate as a chain of signifiers masking or destabilizing the supposed grounds (or transcendent signifieds) of various organizing identities that her detractors want to assign her or between which she wants to fluctuate. This play of identity is conversely related to a process within the lynching issue in which "the rape charge" served a "masking function" for the racist grounds on which segregation and lynching rested.[64] As Robyn Wiegman helpfully explains, "a feminist politics of antiracist struggle . . . is not simply invested in bringing the black woman into critical view but [in] trac[ing] the historical and theoretical contexts that shape her absence and that speak more broadly to the intertwining relationship between patriarchy and white supremacy."[65] The relationship between patriarchy, white supremacy, and black female identity are apparent in Wells's performances as an antilynching agitator abroad, through which she challenges essentialist notions about her identity (and thus emphasizes its fluid nature) and exposes the masked patriarchal and racist grounds for segregationist thinking in the United States.

As Wells's body takes on the cultural weight of various identities, it becomes clear that they not only weigh her down but also mobilize her, since they are the means through which she places her body into circulation. Transatlantic travel propels the body of the writer and text, supplying Wells with opportunities to function as an unrooted body in transit between continents and identities. The relationship between Wells, the writer, who is actually in motion, and the way that motion is inscribed in the text aesthetically and culturally, emphasizes the passages of black transatlantic history on which her travels and texts rest. History is always already lurking in the background of Wells's travel texts, both exposed and elided. Even in the process of denying tourist culture (which would include history as spectacle), she evokes history, but in ways more strategic and transformative than those of a traveler such as Washington.

Traveling through space and history across transatlantic routes both past and present, Wells invokes and complicates the narratives and histories of slavery, segregation, and lynching. In her article of June 25, 1894, Wells notes that women are not allowed on the floor of the British House of Commons, but must stand in the ladies' gallery behind a "cage" of wire netting barring their access. This image of women caged and segregated recurs in a more horrific form in her description of an African American woman "boxed up in [a] barrel into which nails had been driven and rolled down hill in Texas."[66] This link between the British Parliament's segregationist policies and the particularly cruel murder of the Texas woman in a sort of lynching cage allows Wells to critique the various cultural cages of segregation. Furthermore, in the image of the cage we find echoes of slavery's devices of torture and containment with which the literature of slavery and conquest is replete, from J. Hector St. Jean de Crèvecoeur's "man in a cage" in *Letters from an American Farmer* (1782) to the iron muzzles and shackles of Equiano's *Interesting Narrative,* and the "garretted" existence of Harriet Jacobs / Linda Brent in *Incidents in the Life of a Slave Girl* (1861).[67]

By manipulating the tropes of history and travel, Wells embraces the shifting surfaces and essences of black female identity. Describing the contours of this complicated subjectivity, Spillers writes, "I am a marked woman . . . a locus of confounded identities . . . so loaded with mythical prepossession that there is no easy way for the agents buried beneath them to come clean." She continues, "In order for me to speak a truer word concerning myself, I must strip down through layers of attenuated meanings, made an excess . . . over time, assigned by a particular historical order, and there await whatever marvels of my own inventiveness."[68] Wells enacts this unearthing (and, on occasion, masking) by way of her travel experiences, demonstrating that subjectivity is as mobile as the ships of the Middle Passage, the image of which, as Gilroy notes, focuses our attention on the "circulation of ideas" and people in the transatlantic world.[69] Schechter calls attention to the shifting terrain of Wells's project and body when she notes that "Wells's efforts against lynching shed light on the ways in which black bodies became the site of a shifting contest over civil rights and physical integrity, over human dignity and social power. The body in question, whether that of the lynching victim or the African American woman critic, was impossible to represent as a state of biological fixity demanded by Americans to bring order to an uncertain world."[70] Wells embodies this refusal to be fixed not only in her own subjectivity but also in her mobility as a traveler and travel writer as she moves through time and physical space.

She extends these principles of instability to her project of shifting the very ground out from under preconceived notions about segregation. Wells's linking of her own embodied subjectivity to the segregation issue reveals how, to borrow Stuart Hall's words, "identity is formed at the unstable point where the 'unspeakable' stories of subjectivity meet the narratives of history, of a culture."[71] Significantly, Wells manages to speak from the unstable point at which she combines the unspeakable stories of lynching with the histories of segregation. She achieves this voice in the act of traveling and rewriting a colonizing history in which the black woman, heretofore mobilized as slave and captive, now travels as the embodied eyewitness of historical trauma in resistance to contemporary injustice. In doing so, Wells reveals, in Spillers's words, the potential for the African American woman to acquire "the *insurgent* ground as female social subject" and "rewrite after all a radically different text for a female empowerment."[72]

When such "redemptive critique" is read within the context of other black travel narratives less focused on travel's cultural work, we can better appreciate how Wells's complex transatlantic perspective contributed, literally and metaphorically, to the brave rhetoric of her antilynching narratives and, more broadly, to antisegregation arguments in the late nineteenth century. This transatlantic distance emphasizes the increased mobility of post-emancipation African Americans and, in Griffin and Fish's terms, allows Wells to reimagine black mobility and subjectivity in a way that would expand options for improving the status and identities of African Americans in the late nineteenth century. If there is finally any stable ground underneath Wells's embodied performances of subjectivity and segregation, it rests on the facts around which she organizes her final dispatch of July 7, 1894, in which she writes that "all the vile epithets in the vocabulary nor reckless statements cannot change the lynching record of 1893." She concludes by quoting from her own piece published in the *Inter-Ocean* two weeks before: "If I am become an adventuress for simply stating facts, by what name must be characterized those who furnish these facts? However revolting these lynchings, I did not perform a single one of them, nor could the wildest effort of my imagination manufacture one to equal the reality. If the same zeal to excuse and conceal the acts were exercised to put a stop to these lynchings, there would be no need for me to relate nor for the English press to give ear to these tales of barbarity."[73] In this statement she claims the authority to speak truth to segregation's lies, the power to expose those who perpetuate racial violence, and the right to name them according to their vile actions. The imperative to do so becomes part of her important cultural work in the United Kingdom and is sustained by her own position as an embodied eyewitness and traveler.

2

SOUTHERNIZING TRAVEL IN THE BLACK ATLANTIC

Booker T. Washington's *The Man Farthest Down*

In *The Man Farthest Down* (1912), Booker T. Washington demonstrates the cultural and aesthetic negotiations germane to early twentieth-century black travel narratives and illuminates the critical tensions in these texts between mobility and identity that critics such as Farah J. Griffin, Cheryl J. Fish, and Alasdair Pettinger discuss,[1] issues important within the context of current scholarly work in black transatlantic studies. Critical attention to the text has been limited,[2] but *The Man Farthest Down* deserves our renewed attention because it reveals the transatlantic dimensions of what Houston A. Baker Jr. and Dana D. Nelson term "a new Southern studies." Baker and Nelson have argued that "as a nation, we are always already in 'The South,'" and *The Man Farthest Down* represents an important transatlantic extension of this notion, what we might term "Out South," to borrow and expand John Oliver Killens's notion of the United States as "a Southern country," geographically and culturally "Down South" or "Up South."[3]

The Man Farthest Down replicates much of Washington's educational philosophy found in *Up from Slavery* (1901)[4] and other writings, but its critical value is best measured by the ideological conflicts it illuminates, which are tied to Washington's engagement with issues of tourist culture and mobility, racial uplift, and the specter of the South. Undoubtedly Washington's position on black issues was complicated by the fact that he undertook his travel and writing amidst the increased anti-black sentiments created in the South by Thomas Dixon's novels *The Leopard's Spots* (1902) and *The Clansman* (1905),[5] which, as St. Clair Drake reminds us, were both enjoying mass popularity as Washington departed for Europe. Given this social context, Drake argues that *The Man Farthest Down* attests to Washington's "latent intellectual abilities that had to be sacrificed in the interest of institution building and which were obscured by the necessity to wear the mask of an accommodationist leader in a racist society."[6] This context explains what Louis R. Harlan calls Washington's political realism, as well as his contradictory responses to segregation, resulting in policies that were, according to Kevern Verney, "at best often an exercise in damage limitation."[7]

Ultimately, however, Washington's position on black issues complicates his ability to reimagine black travel in a way that would improve the social and political power of African Americans in the early twentieth century and prevents the text from achieving what Paul Gilroy has identified as the "redemptive critique" of modernity and history that represents, aesthetically, the black Atlantic's transformative potential.[8] As with texts before and after emancipation, such as John Pendleton Kennedy's *Swallow Barn* (1832) and Thomas Nelson Page's *In Ole Virginia* (1887), *The Man Farthest Down* projects a sanitized version of the Old South and ignores the horrors of slavery to privilege a southern agrarian home.[9] Washington achieves this result by using the lessons of his European trip to sustain his definitions of work and progress at Tuskegee Institute; thus, instead of revising the meaning of travel for African Americans in the early twentieth century, he essentially rewrites the plantation, replicating the historical plantation's importation of transatlantic labor, products, and ideologies to sustain Old South ideals.

Washington's journey begins when he receives a two-month leave of absence from Tuskegee "on condition that [he] would spend that time in some way that would give [him] recreation and rest."[10] This mandate encourages him to pursue the pleasure-seeking journey of the tourist, as on his first trip to Europe in 1899, which Washington characterized in *Up from Slavery* as a vacation designed to provide him and his wife with much-needed rest. As the ship departed for this earlier journey, Washington felt the cares and burdens of his work lift at a rate of "a pound a minute," and during the trip, he claims that he turned down many invitations to speak because such work would defeat the "object" of his visit. Although Washington managed to draw parallels in *Up from Slavery* between his European experiences and his work, noting in Paris, for example, how the African American artist Henry C. Tanner confirmed the Tuskegee ideal "that any man, regardless of colour, will be recognized and rewarded just in proportion as he learns to do something well . . . however humble the thing may be," the Washingtons also spent a good deal of time enjoying the pleasures of Europe and being entertained by nobility, including Queen Victoria.[11]

During his later European trip detailed in *The Man Farthest Down,* however, and similarly to Wells, Washington maintains that he must abandon the role of tourist in order to become acquainted with the life and condition of Europe's working classes. Like other travel writers of the early twentieth century, Washington describes the method and purpose of his journey within the first few pages of his travel narrative, noting that to promote racial uplift in the South, he studied the methods used to "uplift the masses" of Europe, certain that if he traveled "far enough and deep enough," he would find many European laborers in conditions resembling those of southern blacks. Washington is explicit about the focus of his observations, as well as his preconceptions and agenda, claiming, "I was looking in all the different countries I visited for one class of facts and seeking to make myself familiar with merely one phase of life." He believes that the value of the text lies "not so much in the facts themselves, as in the attempt to bring them together into a single point of view,"[12] suggesting the sort of overarching theory or master narrative that Pettinger warns against,[13] and accomplished through his explicit rejection of tourist culture: "The most difficult things to see are not the sights that every one goes to look at, but the commonplace things that no one sees. In order to carry out the plan I had in mind it was necessary for me to leave the ordinary beaten track of European travel and to plunge into regions which have not been charted and mapped, and where ordinary guides and guide-books are of little or no avail." Resisting what he terms the "conspiracy" of tourist culture that "compel[s]" him to waste his energy on the dead and unchangeable past found in cathedrals, museums, cemeteries, and ruins, he seeks "the new, the unfinished and problematic" amid "the grime and dirt of everyday life" and in the unmapped spaces not yet infiltrated by tourist culture.[14]

These statements contrast with the agendas and perspectives of Washington's white fellow travelers. In 1902 Lyman Abbott, who was the editor of *The Outlook* when portions of *The Man Farthest Down* were serialized in the periodical in 1911 and, in Louis R. Harlan's words, one of Washington's important "white journalist allies,"[15] embraced his role as a leisure traveler, writing in the opening lines of his European travel text *Impressions of a Careless Traveler* (1907) that he was determined to avoid studying not only "art, or architecture, or politics, or literature" in Europe, but also "geography" and "the manners and customs of the people," to "only see what chance and inclination combine to put before my eyes" and "be conscientiously idle."[16] Similarly, in *A Traveler at Forty* (1913), Theodore Dreiser portrayed himself as a carefree traveler with no preconceptions or set agenda as he embarked on his 1911–12 European tour[17] though the text itself refutes his claims of objectivity.

Washington seems to reject tourist culture, and in doing so distinguishes himself from white leisure travelers, yet passages such as the one just quoted, in which he proclaims his preference for uncharted spaces over tourist sites, also reveal his selective use of history in the narrative. Washington's disregard for European history recalls his avoidance of African American history, while his desire "to plunge into regions which have not been charted and mapped" invokes colonialist history and perspective by employing the rhetoric of exploration and conquest, a strategy that Matthew Henson also uses in his travel narrative. By way of such rhetoric, Africa is portrayed in colonial texts such as Conrad's *Heart of Darkness* (1899) as "a blank space" on a map, "a white patch for a boy to dream gloriously over," and which, after being "filled . . . with rivers and lakes and names," becomes a "place of darkness."[18] Although Dickson D. Bruce Jr. has noted that Washington often "play[ed] on white stereotypes of African-Americans . . . to frame his own descriptions" of white European culture and conditions and "to subvert the concept of race,"[19] this reference to unmapped territories carries literary and cultural associations, particularly within the context of the black Atlantic, rendering it more complicit in than subversive of dominant racial ideologies.

At the same time, Washington distinguishes his travels from the adventurous, spectacle-driven journeys detailed in other black travel texts during the period. Like Wells, who, in her 1894 articles on London for the *Chicago Inter-Ocean,* noted that she was too busy alerting readers to the problems of discrimination and the horrors of lynching to act the tourist at the British Museum or Westminster Abbey (though she does appreciate London's "charm of antiquity and historic association"),[20] Washington resists both the touristic and the fantastic by characterizing his journey to see the "commonplace things" of Europe as a working trip that supports his Tuskegee project. Indeed, Washington attempts to rewrite the meaning of transatlantic travel for African Americans and, in the process, recast the meanings of the historic Middle Passage by looking past these defining routes and experiences of slavery's bondage, labor, and narratives to emphasize his project of racial uplift for southern blacks. This new definition of cultural work, exemplified by Tuskegee, is sustained through his interpretation of working conditions in Europe.

While Washington's plan for an optimistic future based on industrial education seems deliberately designed to look beyond slavery's past, such a perspective implies both a literal and psychological return to the plantation, as Baker has observed.[21] Indeed, Washington "imports" ideas and experiences from his European trip in order to sustain his work at Tuskegee, an act that parallels the historical plantation's reliance, as James Walvin has noted, on "massive and continuing imports from across the Atlantic"[22] and suggests Washington's concurrence with some of the ideologies supporting the Atlantic slave trade. Tuskegee Institute, Baker reminds us, was located out of town on a plantation "abandoned by whites in favor of more profitable southern business enterprises such as lumbering" and was established on the principles of "black peasant southern plantation economics, manners, handicrafts, and habits of mind . . . that had been hallmarks of plantation black abjection under southern slavery." Washington's school becomes a "redacted *plantation,*" says Baker, "forestalling rather than fostering mobility of the black-South body beyond or out of abjection," a " 'retrofitting' of black American life in the New South."[23] Washington reads his European experience within the frame of the post-Reconstruction retrofitting to which Baker refers.

His determination to avoid the relics of history parallels his plan for racial uplift, which is to turn away and "up" from slavery's past toward a new economic future for African Americans through industrial education, and he vilifies tourist culture to attain his point. For example, contrasting the "splendid panorama of the beautiful bay of Palermo" with the squalor of Sicily's interior regions, Washington notes that the regular experience of leisure travel is superficially visual and picture-like, and one must penetrate both in (physically) and down (socially) to get a sense of the culture. Europe "looks better on the outside than it looks on the in," and the real life of a country lies past both the "pictures" of travel and the relics of history. East London, he observes, "has no monuments, . . . theatres, art galleries," and, finally, "no history," but it does have "poverty" and "problems," the "interesting and attractive" elements on which his research into "the man farthest down" depends. Throughout the narrative Washington relies on this dichotomy between real life and historical/tourist spectacle to argue that the "greatest boon" for the European laborer (and, by extension, blacks) is to have "steady work" and to receive an industrial education.[24]

By insisting on the significance and nobility of the man farthest down, Washington invokes class issues central to his argument in earlier texts. For example, Andreá N. Williams has noted the important class distinctions that Washington makes in his 1903 essay "Industrial Education for the Negro," in which he emphasizes the difference between the "degradation" of "being worked" and the elevated status of "working," an important component of his pragmatic argument that physical work rather than political enfranchisement was key to the economic progress of African Americans and the South. His insistence on the nobility and honor of labor, which Williams finds reminiscent of a similar emphasis in William Wells Brown and Frederick Douglass,[25] played well with his white audiences and allowed him to underscore in *The Man Farthest Down* the superior conditions of southern black laborers in the United States.

Washington furthers his argument for industrial education when he comes in contact with what he calls the "woman problem," child labor, and slave emancipation in the West Indies. The specific threats to subjectivity posed by slavery-like working conditions and the expanded options for self-understanding made possible by emancipation receive less emphasis in the text than the issues of labor and education that such conditions and events illuminate. In regard to conditions for women, he concludes that "in Europe the man farthest down is woman," because of a lack of industrial education. Washington believes that the women of Prague, for example, do much more rough and unskilled work than Negro women because they are not taught a skill, and he notes that, unlike Italian women, "every Negro girl in America has the same opportunities for education that are given to Negro boys. She may enter the industrial school, or she may, if she choose[s] . . . go to college. All the trades and the professions are open to her." Child labor is also evident in Italy, and he is shocked at the treatment of young boys in the sulfur mines, observing that "the cruelties to which the child slaves have been subjected, as related by those who have studied them, are as bad as anything that was ever reported of the cruelties of Negro slavery." But he downplays the horrors of such practices when he insists that because Italian children are trained in a trade through an apprentice system, "an industrial education such as no other kind of school can give," they ultimately have an advantage over American blacks, an argument which, taken to its logical conclusions, might even suggest that blacks learned more on the plantation than in freedom.[26]

He uses a similar narrative strategy earlier in the text when, near London, he tours Waltham Abbey, the county seat of Sir T. Foxwell Buxton, grandson and namesake of the man who framed the bill emancipating slaves in the English West Indies. Washington's narrative neglect of the emancipation reveals that he is more taken with the rural spectacle, the way the "flowering vines cover the humble cottage of the farm labourer as well as the luxurious country seats of the landowners, and lend a charm to everything the eye rests upon," than with the important struggle for freedom suggested by Buxton's family history and the increased opportunities for mobility and self-creation that this legislation provided to ex-slaves or the political implications of such social history for American blacks. Indeed, while he devotes a chapter to describing Europe's radicalized lower classes, who used strikes, labor unions, and cooperative societies to achieve the same goals for which he was working, he gives little thought to the potential for such activism in the southern United States.[27]

In fact, Washington enacts a complex and often contradictory strategy of accommodation and resistance in *The Man Farthest Down,* "cleaning up" the plantation and lifting up the act of labor in his discussion of black southern life and European agriculture, while simultaneously opposing racial violence, particularly lynching, and promoting black professional-managerial culture in other writings, as I discuss later in this chapter. Predictably, given the references to cleanliness in his autobiography, where Washington famously acquires entrance to Hampton Institute because of his ability to clean,[28] the sight of the drab and commonplace in Europe stimulates his nostalgic longing for the color, laughter, and cleanliness of black southern life. Observing, on a Sunday morning, the "motley" and "ill-dressed" crowds in London's Jewish quarter, he notes that southern blacks, at least, will "put on a clean collar or a bright necktie or something out of the ordinary out of respect for the Sabbath." Even in small one-room cabins on southern plantations, Washington remarks, there is "some evidence of an effort to be tidy."[29] Several years after making these observations, Washington would promote "the application of modern methods of sanitation" and health education as the best means to prevent sickness (and thus idleness) among black southern workers, noting that such a campaign now among rural blacks would curtail the need later, as he had witnessed in English cities, "to rescue drunkards, gamblers, [and] loafers."[30] Washington's urge to prevent or clean up the "dirt" of black southern life emphasizes the relationship, in his mind, between white purity/innocence and black impurity/sexuality, which prompts him, as Baker has observed, to promote a life of agrarian simplicity in order to counteract the desire "to escape manual labor and the soil" and to contain the "dirt" and disorder of the black libidinous body by institutionalizing, at Tuskegee, "the sanitizing of such desires."[31]

Washington's project of sanitizing and uplifting depends on a "cleaned-up" version of his southern past. For example, his experience with Sicilians, who, he concludes, spend too much time wallowing in their past, suggests that in comparison the Negro is not the man farthest down. Yet the charm of the Sicilian wine harvest evokes Washington's own past through boyhood memories of slaves husking corn on the plantation; when the leader of the wine harvest sings, in particular, it reminds him of the leader of the southern corn husking, a man with head bowed and hands pressed against his temples, "listening to music that welled up inside of him," and then "suddenly fling[ing] back his head and burst[ing] into a wilder and more thrilling strain." Washington invokes the blues of African American experience but, through nostalgia, sanitizes the immense despair of the blues song in order to lift up the act of labor. Similarly, rumors of underground revolution in Russia remind him, he says, of "the stories I had heard, when I was a boy, from my mother's lips of the American Underground Railway and the adventures of the runaway slaves in their efforts to cross the border between the free and slave states. It reminded me, also, of the wilder and more desperate struggles, of which we used to hear whispers in slavery time, when the slaves sought to gain their freedom by means of insurrection."[32] By cleaning up these stories and presenting them as "adventures" rather than life-threatening horrors, and by approaching these events from within the context of a childhood memory, he distances himself from the whispered tales of terror and insurrection shared by older slave men and women.

Ultimately, however, the grime of everyday life can sometimes be too dirty; at the wine harvest, his sentimental journey into boyhood memory ends when he recognizes that he has little desire to drink wine from grapes trampled by workers' feet. "It perhaps would not have been so bad," he says, "if the men had not worn their socks."[33] Though Washington believes that history's superficial spectacles–cum–tourist attractions detract from the real cultural lessons to be learned in Europe, it becomes clear that his fraught visions of Europe and the agrarian South (constituting what Basil Mathews characterizes as "the incessant swing of . . . [Washington's] imagination to and fro between the life of the European and that of the American Negro") do not engender a social discourse that empowers southern blacks.[34]

A nostalgia for the southern plantation also surfaces in Washington's text through his fascination with the tools of European agriculture. While he believes that the future of European peasants and southern blacks depends on agricultural education and forward thinking, he also invokes the historical plantation through his interest in the ancient tools of agriculture. He admires the ruins of Sicily but notes that the region's agricultural implements and methods, referred to in his travel guidebooks, are even older (and, implicitly, more worthy of the traveler's attention) than the ruins.[35] Utilizing the criteria of the tourist, Washington romanticizes these "living" relics of labor as tourist spectacle, which, like ruins of "southern plantation economics, manners, handicrafts, and habits of mind,"[36] invoke, as C. Vann Woodward observes, the "brickmaking, blacksmithing, wheelwrighting, harness making, basketry, [and] tin-smithing" of both Tuskegee and the Old South.[37] Washington sees antique wooden plows, possibly like those mentioned in Homer, "a wine press . . . as old as Solomon," winemaking methods "described in the Bible," and herdsmen tending their goats and cows, "counting the stars as the shepherds did in the time of Abraham," and concludes that the people of Sicily are "so saturated with antiquity . . . it would take a very long time . . . to get any understanding of their ways of thinking and living." Washington experiences an intriguing tension here between his fascination with and avoidance of history, for though Sicily suggests to him the importance of going back in history in order to understand the present,[38] we know from his reworking of slavery's history and his romanticizing of the agrarian South that for him the value of such understanding is contingent on its usefulness within the context of his political agenda.

Washington's avoidance of African American history becomes a rhetorical pose that produces in the text a particular historical representation of his ideal reader. The complexity of his approach was also part of his own historical significance as a writer, an educator, and, despite his objections to the contrary, a politically active race man. In this light, Washington's glorification of black women's educational opportunities in *The Man Farthest Down,* as noted earlier, functions as a rhetorical device designed to market interest, solicit sympathy, and generate money for Tuskegee. Indeed, Harlan notes that Washington responded to requests from white employers for students to serve as domestics by reiterating Tuskegee's philosophy of preparing black women to use their education within the black households and communities of the South,[39] thus avoiding the problems of wage labor that he observed among European peasants and with which his white audience would most likely have been familiar. In his 1910 *Good Housekeeping* magazine article "Teaching Domestic Economy at Tuskegee," Washington emphasizes this philosophy to the magazine's mostly white audience, claiming that Tuskegee "has a double problem": not only to train its students in a vocation but also "to change the conditions of life which surround the masses of the negro people."[40]

Washington's support of the antilynching movement and his emphasis on black managerial culture offer further evidence of his complex relationship with his audience. The record of lynching incidents, which Washington and his personal secretary, Emmet Scott, kept at Tuskegee from 1899 to 1915, including the extensive file of newspaper clippings detailing such events,[41] attests to his antilynching sentiments. By lifting up the lynched black body, Washington aligns himself politically with the kind of movement that he publicly avoided in the interest of maintaining white sympathy; but his writing on the issue, what we could perhaps consider the public voice he lends to his private horror, stages a dialectic of resistance and accommodation.

Washington keeps his earlier statements on lynching appropriately acquiescent, ever aware, as Baker observes, of "both the cognitive . . . and somatic . . . screens on which the mind of the South would read black 'manly' public performances."[42] In his November 2, 1901, article "Lynch Law and

Anarchy," published in the *Sunday School Times,* Washington notes that although lynching began as a punishment for rape (he does not address the problems of such punishment), murderers and thieves now constitute a larger percentage of those lynched, and he characterizes lynching as a harbinger of lawlessness linked to idleness and a lack of education.[43] In a July 2, 1903, speech to the National Afro-American Council, Washington also warns that if the law is disregarded when blacks are accused of crimes, then it will not be long before whites are also victims of such lawlessness. (It appears that Washington attached a copy of this speech to a July 7, 1903, letter to Charles Chesnutt in response to Chesnutt's criticism of his preoccupation with "education and property.")[44] His March 29, 1907, address to the theology department at Vanderbilt University is less conciliatory, however. Arguing that lynching gives the South an undeserved reputation for lawlessness and that sexual assault is a national rather than a southern (and black) phenomenon, he gives the example of Chicago, where "two years ago there were more attempts made by white men at rape than there were throughout the whole of the Southern States, so far as the colored people were concerned." In "Is the Negro Having a Fair Chance?" from *The Century* of November 1912, he even observes that whites sometimes "blackened their faces and committed a crime, knowing that some negro would be suspected and mobbed for it."[45]

His critics, however, continued to view his position on lynching as problematic, and during his 1910 European tour, one of Washington's friends, John Elmer Milholland, refused an invitation to dine with Washington, partly because of his unwillingness to "denounce lynching or peonage." In the August 29, 1910, *London Daily Chronicle,* Washington is quoted as saying, "If there is a lynching all the world knows about it next day, but if the coloured people build a college, establish a bank, or a store, or erect houses for themselves, nothing is known about it except in the community." In a November 24, 1910, letter to Washington, William Pickens cautioned him about the misleading nature of his public statements on lynching, observing that the *London Morning Post* claimed "to have gotten the impression from Dr. Washington that the reports of mob violence are greatly exaggerated, and that it is wrong to suppose that the American Negro is suffering,"[46] the latter being an impression that Washington also promotes in *The Man Farthest Down.*

Washington's stance on both lynching and the black business class converge in his August 30, 1906, speech in Atlanta, Georgia, to the National Negro Business League. Claiming that the South is the "best permanent abode" for African Americans, Washington charts the natural progression of black progress in the South: "ownership and cultivation of the soil, the saving of money, commercial growth, and the skillful, conscientious performance of any duty with which we are entrusted." Black business leaders must positively influence degenerate blacks, he observes, for "lynchers and those who provoke lynching" are the greatest detriment to black business success, and only when the race has improved itself from within should it "call upon the whites to do their part."[47] While we must consider the historical context of Washington's statements, remembering that Washington's rhetorical pose in these articles and speeches is often constructed in response to various exigencies (this speech, for example, was delivered as a race riot threatened to break out in the city), it is also important to note the patterns of accommodation that emerge in his public statements and private correspondence about lynching, patterns that recur in his writing on other subjects.

Washington's pairing of black business success with improving the condition and reputation of the race parallels his own rise to success. In a February 1909 article in *World's Work,* he explicitly associates the project of the National Negro Business League with that of Tuskegee,[48] and he suggests in *Leslie's Weekly* in 1908 that business success provides opportunity to turn vegetables and fruit, livestock and cotton "into music, . . . education, [and] . . . high moral living."[49] In *World's Work,* Washington also invokes tropes of cleanliness, essential to his personal history and to his view of black southern life, to note the well-kept and "handsome appearance" of a black drugstore in Natchez, Mississippi.[50] This allusion to the ways in which Washington's own career was launched by his ability to impress a white teacher with his cleanliness reminds us of the white approval on which Washington continued to rely and of the accommodationist stance he pursued to maintain it. Indeed, as Harlan points out, Washington was influenced by the advice of white backers such as John Wanamaker and Andrew Carnegie, who convinced him "that Negroes needed to get out of politics and get into business," and Washington promoted what amounted to commercial segregation in terms of the "special business opportunity" to be found for black business leaders among African Americans in the South.[51] Washington's personal investment in such a program is suggested in his January 1906 article in *American Magazine,* "The Negro in Business" (developed into his book-length treatment of the subject published the following year), containing examples of successful southern black entrepreneurs following a pattern of humble beginnings, perseverance through hardships and setbacks, and the eventual building of a thriving business or even commercial empire, a personal history similar to his own.[52] For Washington, business success seemed to offer a suitable alternative to enfranchisement and also reasserted the central role of the South in black progress.

Clearly, then, Washington viewed his ideal audience not as the white southerners who criticized him for, among other things, not providing them with black domestics but as the northern reform-minded white philanthropists eager to champion (philosophically and financially) his theories of black progress. Favorable reviews of *The Man Farthest Down* further imply the existence of such an audience. For example, the *New York Times Book Review* of October 6, 1912, praises Washington as "a leader of his race rather than its spokesman or champion," who, unlike W. E. B. Du Bois, "wishes to plead with his people rather than for them," and whose chief purpose is "to get them to make the most of themselves under present conditions," and only secondarily to "improve those conditions" rather than agitate for political enfranchisement. The reviewer's northern bias is clearly revealed in a jab aimed at the South: Washington's assertion that blacks are more like the southern white man than like any immigrant group entering the United States is surely a "bitter pill . . . for Southern white men to swallow!"[53]

As noted earlier, much of *The Man Farthest Down* was serialized in *The Outlook,* whose editor, Lyman Abbott, a Congregationalist minister and leading proponent of the Social Gospel movement, lauded Washington's focus on individual improvement and hard work as the root of overall black progress. On September 1, 1906, *The Outlook* expressed a preference for "the more industrial and the more pacific spirit" of Washington and Tuskegee over "the more assertive spirit" of Du Bois's Niagara Movement, noting that the movement "would be more useful if it demanded more of the negro race and put less emphasis on its demands for the negro race." (Washington, in a letter to Abbott dated September 2, 1906, complained that the editorial devoted too much attention to Du Bois.)[54] Similarly, in *Reminiscences* (1915), Abbott claims that Washington's emphasis on black industrial education has elevated the cause of such education and promoted its ideals of service for all Americans. *The Outlook*'s brief notice about *The Man Farthest Down* on October 5, 1912, is likewise laudatory in tone, remarking Washington's "hopeful" and "cheerful" attitude toward

"American industrial life" and casting him as a "fair-minded observer." Edwin Markham, revealing his own interests in labor and reform, also notes in his January 1913 *Heart's Magazine* review that a "book from . . . [Washington's] pen means direct first-hand knowledge, and terse, fair and free discussion" and observes that the text is "an illuminating sociological study of our troubled problems of immigration and labor."[55]

Significantly, the *Outlook* notice clearly acknowledges Washington as the text's chief observer and, unlike the *New York Times* review, does not mention Robert Ezra Park as a collaborator, though Washington refers to this collaboration in the text. In a letter to Park dated October 6, 1912, Washington directed his attention to the positive reviews of the text, particularly to the *Times* review in which Park's role is emphasized.[56] In contrast to its emphasis on Washington as the primary author of his text, *The Outlook*'s March 9, 1912, notice about Matthew Henson's travel narrative of the Peary North Pole expedition, *A Negro Explorer at the North Pole* (1912), states that Henson is a man of "considerable intelligence and some education," but describes the book as a mere "supplement to the complete and full story which his chief [Robert Edwin Peary] has given to the world."[57] At one point in the introduction he wrote for Henson's narrative, Washington himself refers to Henson as Peary's "companion" in exploration (Peary, in his foreword to the text, refers to Henson as a "member" of his expedition), but also situates Henson's "fidelity and devotion" to Peary within a long history of other black men who accompanied great explorers, revealing that "even . . . when the Negro had little or no opportunity to show his ability as a leader, he proved himself at least a splendid follower."[58] As I discuss further in chapter 3, Peary's foreword and Washington's introduction to Henson's narrative ultimately serve a function similar to that of the legitimizing prefatory materials published with slave narratives, implying the inferiority of Henson's account, a point of view that the *Outlook* notice also perpetuates.

A March 30, 1912, *Outlook* editorial, "Some Notable Educational Enterprises: Tuskegee Institute," even more explicitly reveals the magazine's positive editorial bias toward Washington, and in fact reads like an advertisement for the school. The editorial observes that Tuskegee's trustees wish to increase the endowment fund so that Washington and his fellow educators will be able to expend their energy on education rather than fund-raising, provides examples of Tuskegee's educational innovations, and notes that the head of Sears, Roebuck and Company, Julius Rosenwald, has joined the board of trustees, presided over by Seth Low, former president of Columbia University. The editorial concludes with the hope that "the contributions to the Tuskegee endowment fund from Northern benefactors will be generous."[59]

Washington's favorable reception among white philanthropic audiences serves to emphasize his problematic collaboration with his informal secretary, Robert Ezra Park, a collaboration that further demonstrates his troubled relationship with racial history by invoking the slave past and complicating his efforts to reimagine the European grand tour. Although Washington's travel text does not contain the editorial preface and afterword between which slave narratives are often sandwiched, Park's white authorial presence permeates the text, compromising Washington's narrative authority. Park is the white sociologist who corroborates, authenticates, and corrects Washington's impressions. Indeed, Park, who eventually acquired a reputation as an authority in racial issues, essentially scripts Washington's travels and his travel narrative.

Although reviews of the text tended to downplay Park's contribution, Park not only accompanied Washington through Europe but also went to Europe some months before Washington "to study the situation," making it possible, writes Washington, "for me to see more in a short space of time than I could otherwise have been able to." Washington claims that he uses Park's observations as much as his own, to the point where he is unable to differentiate between portions of the text based on his own perceptions and those based on Park's.[60] Acting as guide and interpreter, Park procures various documents during the trip, enabling Washington to "correct" his first impressions and "supplement them with the facts and statistics" about what they observe. Park also locates information in bookstores and libraries, which, according to Washington, "straighten[ed] out" and "complete[d]" his ideas, and in the narrative Washington sometimes quotes verbatim from Park's travel notes.[61] While Washington attempts to construct a travel narrative that not only refutes the conventions of leisure travel but also, in its representation of black mobility, implicitly resists the trope of the slave's forced journey, his efforts to rewrite black travel are compromised by the degree to which he relinquishes control of the journey, the sociological work, and the narrative to Park, a loss of control for which he then seems to compensate by refusing to acknowledge Park as co-author.

Washington's narrative also demonstrates the ways in which he depends on Park and other guides for access and mobility. For example, traveling to the mines at Campofranco in southern Sicily, Washington is uneasy about "start[ing] off into a wild region, which no guide-book had charted and, so far as . . . [he] knew, no tourist had ever visited." He is relieved to be with Park, who has an Italian grammar in his satchel and undertakes four hours of study in order to get them through the ordeal. Park's understanding of German allows Washington to speak to a Jewish trader near Kraków, who then volunteers to be his guide to peasant life in the area; Washington declares that "at . . . [the guide's] touch, every door flew open," ensuring him access to peasant homes. In Russia, Park "manage[s] to pick up something of the family histories," which offer Washington insights into the daily life of the community. A guide and interpreter also escorts them in Russian Poland, providing Washington with local gossip from which he gains "a more intimate view" of the society and the benefits of its agricultural base.[62] Washington's perspective, then, is filtered through Park and other individuals who control not only what he sees and hears but also his route and mobility, keeping him metaphorically and ideologically in the Old South.

As we might expect, however, Washington utilizes these mediated interactions with Europe's peasants not only to prove that land and education will move the masses ahead and up but also to emphasize the peasants' ability to lift all other classes above them, implying the important contribution of black southern labor to widespread progress in the United States. Many city problems have their source in the country, he claims, and the best way to improve conditions in the city is to improve conditions in the country, which would also halt the migration from country to city in both America and Europe. Once again drawing on images of southern cleanliness, Washington observes: "It is a great deal simpler and . . . cheaper to . . . develop a people who have grown up in the wholesome air of the open country than it is to regenerate a people who have lived all or most of their lives in the fetid atmosphere of a city slum. In other words, it is easier to deal with people who are physically and morally sound than with people who, by reason of their unhealthy and immoral surroundings, have become demoralized and degenerate." Washington notes that London has spent large amounts of money cleaning up the slums by providing "sunshine, air, and water" (that is, "wider streets, breathing spaces, . . . swimming pools, and washrooms"), which one can have for free in the country (for example, by washing clothes in a brook or fishing and swimming in an "old-fashioned swimming hole"). At great expense, London has created country suburbs to provide an environment similar to what four-fifths of the Negro population already enjoys. Washington suggests that the money would have been better spent improving the conditions in the country through industrial education,[63] implying by this vision of a pastoral utopia, which continues to ignore racial history, that both black and American progress in general also depend on improved health conditions and education in the rural South, an argument that, as noted earlier, he reiterated in his 1914 article "Eugenics and the Negro."

While Washington believes that the European peasant could benefit from a lifestyle similar to that in the American South, he is uncomfortable with the idea of European immigration to the southern United States. Immigrants from southern Europe herd together, he says, becoming more social and less independent than those from the north, and then move to cities when they come to the United States. He argues that a large influx of foreign immigrants to the southern United States would create racial problems more serious than those that now exist. His philosophy of immigration exposes his complicit acceptance of a white identity for African Americans, for, Washington argues, "whatever else one may say of the Negro, he is, in everything except his colour, more like the Southern white man, more willing and able to absorb the ideas and the culture of the white man and adapt himself to existing conditions, than is true of any race which is now coming into this country." European immigration also suggests to Washington the potential effects of African American migration from the rural South to cities. Immigration to the United States threatens the "rising prosperity" of the land in Hungary, and in southern Italy, he argues, "the neglect of the agricultural classes" has caused a mass exodus. By alluding to post-Reconstruction migration to the North and anticipating its eventual effects in the United States, he implies that unless agricultural life and education are made priorities in the American South, many southern blacks will move to the cities, ultimately depleting the South economically and agriculturally.[64]

Reflecting on the meaning of his travel at the end of his journey, Washington implicitly returns to the Old South home threatened by European immigration and black northern migration. In her analysis of the African American migration narrative, Farah Jasmine Griffin notes the ways in which such narratives invoke the South, "not just in its horror, terror, and exploitation, but as a place that housed the values and memories that sustained black people. The South emerges as the home of the ancestor, the place where community and history are valued over Northern individualism."[65] Though not a migration narrative (indeed, it represents a sort of anti-migration narrative), Washington's travel text similarly turns toward a southern home, but one that ignores slavery's horrors to emphasize an agrarian ideal and court white sympathy. As Frances Bartkowski might suggest, Washington has carefully chosen the "place[s], . . . routes, . . . [and] questions" of his travel,[66] attempting to rewrite the meaning of travel in the black Atlantic through the kinds of choices he makes. But his travel choices prevent him from drawing any new conclusions about self or home (what we might expect of travel narratives, according to Bartkowski) and fail to move him away from the historical plantations or ships' holds of the Middle Passage and nearer an expanded notion of black progress and identity. He concludes his narrative by stating that as he traveled among Europe's working classes, he "found . . . [himself] looking at things from the point of view of the people who are looking up, rather than from that of the people who are at the top looking down." To the man in the street, looking up, "the thing he aims at and is striving toward stands out clear and distinct above him, inspiring him with hope and ambition in his struggle upward." Indeed, "the man who is down, looking up, may catch a glimpse now and then of heaven."[67]

At the conclusion of Washington's transatlantic travels, then, we find him looking up into the southern past. Although, as Winifred Raushenbush and others have suggested, Washington's experiences in Europe may have allowed him to think more progressively about civil rights in his later years,[68] such a view is not substantiated in *The Man Farthest Down,* where he relies on narrative strategies also apparent in his writing on other black issues to privilege his specific view of black uplift while downplaying the material realities of racial history.[69] And while he attempts, at least in theory, to avoid the lure of tourism experienced by Douglass, Merriman-Labor, and Seacole, such efforts do not lead to an expanded view of personal, racial, or political identity for African Americans, revealing that despite having traveled through Europe for seven weeks, Washington never left the South.

3

"TO RETURN AND TELL THE TALE OF THE DOING"

Matthew Henson and the African American Explorer's Identity

While also contending with the limiting forces of the slave narrative form, Matthew Henson is more successful than Washington in asserting the empowering nature of black identity and mobility in his travel writing. Near the end of *A Negro Explorer at the North Pole* (1912), Henson describes his discovery of the North Pole with Commander Robert Peary on April 6, 1909, characterizing it as a moment of "savage joy and exultation." Utilizing the language of exploration and conquest, Henson notes that "another world's accomplishment was done and finished, and as in the past, from the beginning of history, wherever the world's work was done by a white man, he had been accompanied by a colored man." After a brief recounting of the event, Henson adds, "The long trail was finished, the work was done, and there was only left for us to return and tell the tale of the doing."[1] On one hand, Henson's statement reflects the general motive of most travel narratives: to recount the journey once it is complete. But the narration of Henson's journey is more complicated than his brief statement implies; indeed, he enacts a complex negotiation of identity as an African American explorer, relying on concepts of authority, mobility, and subjectivity associated with the genre of the exploration narrative while resisting the cultural ideologies of the slave narrative.

Throughout the text, Henson represents himself at various times as equal, superior, or subordinate to Peary. His willingness to characterize himself in a subordinate position suggests the master-slave dichotomy, which is emphasized in other ways in the text, as I will demonstrate. The fact that he refers to his journey as "work," and the narrative as a tale of "doing" rather than of leisure or pleasure, underscores the influence of both the slave and exploration narratives on the text while calling attention to the cultural work that his narrative undertakes. Alluding to such work, Tim Youngs argues that by challenging geographical, racial, and textual restrictions, African American "travel and its textual representation combine to create a space in which identity can be affirmed, discovered, or renegotiated."[2] In his narrative Henson engages with the discovery and negotiation of his identity as an explorer which is in some ways denied him by the apparatus of the text itself, for example, in the introduction and foreword, which emphasize his role as subordinate to Peary and call his agency into question. Henson's narrative does not neatly fit into either the slave or the exploration narrative genre, both of which are diverse in their own right, but the tensions in Henson's text between these two genres allow him to challenge conventional notions about the explorer's identity, illuminating the important cultural work performed by African American travel narratives during the age of Jim Crow.

Henson published his narrative with Peary's stipulation that he be allowed to review the manuscript first.[3] The book appeared with a foreword by Peary, who characterized Henson as a credit to his race. As I discussed in chapter 2, Booker T. Washington also wrote a brief introduction for the text, noting that Henson was the "most trusted" and "useful member of the expedition" and that he was "not the first colored man who by his fidelity and devotion has made himself the trusty companion of the men who have explored . . . the western continent." Washington explicitly connects the work of exploration to black fidelity and trustworthiness, noting Peary's reference to Henson's loyalty as a reason why he entrusted him with so much responsibility and claiming that "even in the days when the Negro had little or no opportunity to show his ability as a leader, he proved himself at least a splendid follower, and there are few great adventures in which the American white man has engaged where he has not been accompanied by a colored man." Washington provides examples demonstrating that most early Spanish explorers were assisted by blacks and ends his introduction by stating that Henson "has proven again that courage, fidelity, and ability are honored and rewarded under a black skin as well as under a white."[4]

This framing of a black text through prefatory material recalls the rhetoric and design of slave narratives containing introductions or testimonials, usually written by white men and meant, as James Olney observes, to legitimize the text. Olney suggests that the statement "I was born," which begins many slave narratives, also served to validate the existence and identity of the writer, and he argues that the slave narrative's "claim of truthfulness" and authenticity is secondary to this primary claim, "I exist."[5] Within the first few paragraphs of his narrative, Henson employs this same strategy as a validating device, even though he was born just after the Civil War. The fourth paragraph of his narrative begins: "I was born in Charles County, Maryland, August 8, 1866. The place of my birth was on the Potomac River, about forty-four miles below Washington, D.C. Slavery days were over forever when I was born. Besides, my parents were both free born before me, and in my mother's veins ran some white blood."[6] Several features of this biographical statement are significant. First, though Henson was born just after slavery ended, he emphasizes that both of his parents were freeborn, further distancing himself from the taint of slavery. Yet he combines this information about his parents' free status with the fact that his mother was partly white. The reference seems ironic, given that mixed-race parentage usually indicated the rape of female slaves, so one might think that such a reference would invoke the horrors of rather than the freedom from slavery. The fact that his identification of his mother's race is combined with the statement that his parents were born free might suggest that he equates whiteness with freedom, though there are other moments in the text when he seems more critical of whiteness and what it represents, as I discuss later in this chapter. The racial details of these validating introductions and biographical statements simultaneously invoke and undermine slave narrative form and ideology.

Another formal characteristic of the slave narrative in Henson's text is his emphasis on his literacy. The titles of slave narratives, often containing the phrase "written by himself" or "related by herself" (as in the case of Olaudah Equiano, Frederick Douglass, and Mary Prince), highlight the feats of literacy contained therein. Henson shows the sophistication of his literacy through references to Shakespeare, Dickens, Alexander the Great, and the Bible. He reports that he brings with him on the journey volumes by Dickens, Kipling, and Thomas Hood, as well as Peary's books on the Arctic, and notes that on the ship, he and his companions set up a sort of "circulating library."[7] Such references correspond to instances in slave narratives when the authors quote literature or philosophy to demonstrate literacy. In contrast to the slave narrative convention of documenting the barriers to literacy or describing the lengths to which one might go to acquire literacy—for example, Frederick Douglass tricking white boys into helping him learn the letters of the alphabet and copying out his young master's copybook when left in the house by himself—Henson's references to literature demonstrate that not even the rigors of the Arctic trail can keep him from his literate pursuits.[8]

Henson's references to the Bible and his insistence that he reads it as regularly as his work allows parallel the emphasis in many slave narratives and their prefaces on the slave's Christian devotion, further proof of the account's validity. Olaudah Equiano's *Interesting Narrative* (1789) provides a compelling example of this feature. Equiano, who also made an Arctic voyage in the eighteenth century, notes that the journey took four months, "in which time, at the imminent hazard of our lives, we explored nearly as far towards the Pole as 81 degrees north, and 20 degrees east longitude; being much farther, by all accounts, than any navigator had ever ventured before." In the preface, Equiano addresses "the Lords spiritual and temporal, and the Commons of the Parliament of Great Britain," observing that, although "by the horrors" of the slave trade he has been "torn away from all the tender connections that were naturally dear to [his] heart," he "ought to regard" these atrocities as "infinitely more than compensated by the introduction [he has] thence obtained to the knowledge of the Christian religion, and of a nation which, by its liberal sentiments, its humanity, the glorious freedom of its government, and its proficiency in arts and sciences, has exalted the dignity of human nature."[9] Though Equiano's statement seems to be a model of accommodation, it is also an apt example of veiled cultural critique. Indeed, his ambivalent statement that he "ought to regard" his horrific experience as more than compensated for by his introduction to Christianity suggests that he may not harbor such feelings at all but is instead signifying on the idea that his captors or the government officials to whom he addresses the preface would consider such compensation sufficient for his hardships.

Another prominent feature of the slave narrative is the author's tendency to speak of his or her hard work. Henson describes at length the difficult labor of breaking trail and repairing sledges. At one point he combines both a biblical reference (to demonstrate his piety, trustworthiness, and literacy) and his work ethic in a scene in which he is kept busy adjusting the loads of the sleds until well into the evening and, while doing so, comes across his Bible. Before going to bed that night, he reads the twenty-third Psalm and the fifth chapter of the Book of Matthew.[10] Henson effectively uses these elements of the slave narrative—that is, an emphasis on Christian devotion, literacy, and hard work—to characterize himself in the best light. He also participates in the sort of veiled cultural critique seen in Equiano's narrative in the sense that he represents himself as performing the menial labor of the journey while working harder than other members of the expedition when he locates his Bible on the sled. In casting himself as more literate, religious, and hardworking than the white members of the expedition, Henson undermines the stereotypes about African American character and culture with which Equiano also contended. This veiled critique, what Anthony S. Foy refers to as Henson's "cunning indirection,"[11] and perhaps similar in some ways to Washington's focus on his own hard work and that of his fellow African Americans, is further evidence of the rhetorical strategies black travel writers adopted in the Jim Crow era in order to resist the period's social limitations.

As a further challenge to the confining cultural, structural, and linguistic forces of both the slave narrative form and the Jim Crow context in which he writes his narrative, Henson stages an interesting dialectic between his identity as Peary's assistant and his status as an explorer in his own right, and he does so by drawing upon features of the exploration narrative.[12] Somewhat ironically, Washington's introduction establishes Henson's status as assistant more thoroughly than Peary's foreword. In Peary's own account of the Pole discovery, he characterizes Henson as both subordinate and expert in various fields. A document Peary left at the pole, listing members of his Arctic Club North Pole Expedition, names Henson as an assistant, but in his narrative he refers to Henson at various times as his "negro assistant," an Eskimo interpreter, or an instructor of igloo construction. Peary also offers an explanation for his inclusion of Henson as a member of the expedition, insisting that by selecting Henson as his "fellow traveler," he "acted exactly as [he had] done on all [his] expeditions for the last fifteen years."[13] Peary's defense of his decision seems intended to emphasize that he followed precedent, and perhaps to ward off some of the public criticism he received for including an African American as a member of the party.

Lowell Thomas notes in his 1939 interview with Henson that Peary was publicly censured because he did not take one of his white assistants on the day of the actual discovery of the pole instead of Henson. Thomas reports, however, that expedition member Donald MacMillan claimed that none of the white team members expected to go to the pole. MacMillan remarked that "Henson was the most useful man of us all," calling him "the best man I've ever seen . . . in the handling of Eskimos." MacMillan resorts to racist stereotype, however, when he notes that "nobody could get along with [Eskimos] as well as Matt Henson. They're a merry people, fond of laughter. Henson, with his flashing white teeth, always had a laugh in his dark face. The Eskimos accepted him almost as one of themselves." He nevertheless concludes that "if ever there was a man who deserves recognition, it's Henson."[14]

Similar to MacMillan, Peary claims in his account of the expedition, *The North Pole: Its Discovery in 1909 under the Auspices of the Peary Arctic Club* (1910), that he took Henson with him because "with his years of arctic experience, [he] was almost as skilful at his work as an Eskimo," and he refers to Henson as "the best man I had with me for this kind of work, with the exception of the Eskimos," statements coinciding with Henson's own assertion of authority as an Arctic traveler and explorer. Yet, like MacMillan, Peary also uses the racialized language of the period to describe Henson's contribution, stating, "[Even though Henson was] faithful to me, and when *with me* more effective in covering distance with a sledge than any of the others, he had not as a racial inheritance, the daring and initiative of Bartlett, or Marvin, MacMillan, or Borup [white members of the expedition]. I owed it to him not to subject him to dangers and responsibilities which he was temperamentally unfit to face."[15] He is willing to characterize Henson as faithful, and even as competent in Arctic exploration, but Peary considers him, as an African American, incapable of accepting responsibility or taking initiative and "temperamentally unfit" to face challenges. The fact that Peary stresses Henson's ability to cover distances in a sledge better than anyone else only when he is *with* him suggests that Peary sees Henson as competent only when he is supervised. Such a comment qualifies the many positive things that Peary says about Henson's abilities.

Peary's assertion of a supervisory position in his relationship with Henson underscores his role as head of the expedition. The significance of this role is emphasized through imperialistic associations and imagery in his own account and in various descriptions of him appearing in the introduction to Peary's *North Pole* by Theodore Roosevelt and the foreword by Gilbert H. Grosvenor. Roosevelt claims that Peary possesses the characteristics that must accompany a successful bid for the pole, such as "great physical hardihood and endurance, an iron will and unflinching courage, the power of command, the thirst for adventure, and a keen and farsighted intelligence,"[16] qualities that Henson undermines when he portrays Peary as disabled and forced to endure much of the journey on a sledge.[17] Roosevelt seems to suggest that Peary has accomplished "one of the great feats of our time" on his own: "He has won high honor for himself and for his country; and we welcome his own story of the triumph which he won in the immense solitudes of the wintry North." Grosvenor, of the National Geographic Society, declares that while some argue "that the glory of Peary's achievement belongs to the world and is shared by all mankind[,] . . . we, his fellow-countrymen, . . . specially rejoice that he has 'made good at last,' and that an American has become the peer of Hudson, Magellan, and Columbus,"[18] again stressing Peary's solo accomplishment.

This emphasis on both individual accomplishment and the imperial agenda is germane to the exploration narrative. Richard Davis observes that exploration literature before World War I "is characterized by a desire . . . to assert the unquestioned supremacy of the human will over undomesticated nature." Exploration narratives during this period revealed explorers' desire to "open up" new territory and to "test themselves against all but impossible hardship" through "tortuous and brutal travel." Davis suggests that such "self-willed tenacity . . . is a part of the unsparing ethos of adventure that grew out of an imperialistic philosophy," emphasizing the pairing of the explorer's personal qualities and larger imperial agendas in these narratives. The goal of exploration is to "dominate [the landscape], to put it on a map, to assign names to its lakes and rivers and mountains"—or, in line with Peary's specific goal in the Arctic, to plant a United States flag in it.[19] Peary left at the pole a glass bottle containing a document dated April 6, 1909, the day of the pole conquest, claiming possession: "I have today hoisted the national ensign of the United States of America at this place, which my observations indicate to be the North Polar axis of the earth, and have formally taken possession of the entire region, and adjacent, for and in the name of the President of the United States of America."[20] Lowell Thomas indicates, however, in his interview with Henson that, according to MacMillan, "it was Henson who placed the Stars and Stripes at the top of the world, while the leader sat exhausted on the sledge and feebly waved his hand,"[21] a portrayal that coincides with Henson's insistence on his active role in the conquest in contrast to Peary's passive participation.

But even if Peary is physically limited, the discourse of exploration privileges his intellectual accomplishments. Davis writes that because "frivolous recreation," or "activity without material accomplishment," was counter to the imperialist endeavor, the explorer had to fulfill "the task of adding to the stores of geographical knowledge."[22] This push to contribute to the imperialist storehouse of knowledge was heightened by what Roy Bridges identifies as the "severe international competition and territorial annexations" of the period from 1880 to 1914, and the "anxiety" accompanying these contests.[23] Henson's brief reference to Peary's competition with Cook over the discovery of the pole and the controversy that ensued reminds us of these contests for geographical dominance.[24] Theodore Roosevelt's comments in his introduction to Peary's *North Pole* characterize the feat as a great *American* conquest. Roosevelt states that "thanks to [Peary] the discovery of the North Pole was to go on the honor roll of those feats in which we take a peculiar pride because they have been performed by our fellow countrymen,"[25] further suggesting the fierce international competition of discovery.

Significantly, none of Henson's geographical observations make it into Peary's account of the pole discovery (Peary includes a second appendix with facsimiles of observations from various team members), an absence which implies that Henson's contribution was chiefly to the physical rather than the intellectual aspects of the journey,[26] though Henson frequently refers in his own narrative to his work of making these observations. In a 1910 article in the *Boston American,* Henson even questions the accuracy of Peary's observations by remarking that because Peary has ridden most of the way, in contrast to walking as Henson and the Eskimos have done, he is unable to judge distances as accurately as Henson. When Peary leaves him repairing a sledge while taking two Eskimos to calculate the position of the pole, Henson reports, "I was sorely disappointed, but somehow I had an abiding faith that he was wrong in his calculations." He challenges Peary, telling him that he, Henson, has kept track of the distance and suspects that they are "at the Pole," adding, "If we have not traveled in the right direction then it is your own fault." According to this account, Peary does not reply but goes off by himself to make observations. Henson writes, "I can make observations myself, but of course, I did not meddle at this time."[27] Henson's characterization of events promotes his own expertise while emphasizing the difficult work of exploration.

Reviews of Henson's text nevertheless imply Peary's dominance and assert the lesser significance of Henson's narrative in comparison to Peary's more authoritative account. A *New York Times* reviewer claims that Henson's "little volume . . . makes a really valuable addition to the literature of Admiral Peary's final, successful expedition" but also characterizes his version as naïve and filled with "innumerable bits of incident, occupation, description, emotion, [and] comment," which "are unimportant in themselves, but they help wonderfully in filling out the picture and in enabling the reader to get a more definite idea of what the life and labors of an arctic explorer are like." The lack of such "little colorful touches" and a concern "with affairs of great moment" in other accounts of polar exploration make these accounts less appealing to readers in comparison to Henson's narrative. While seeming to categorize Henson with other Arctic explorers, the review suggests that, even if enjoyable, his narrative is trivial; indeed, the reviewer states that the book "is a very personal one" with Henson as "the centre of the story." A *Nation* reviewer similarly diminishes the text as "Mr. Henson's little book" and "a narrative of personal impressions . . . marred here and there by bits of passionate prose which one imagines was inserted by another hand other than the author's," though why this would be so, the reviewer does not say. The reviewer also claims that Henson does not give a *complete* account of the journey, by which he or she "means the inclusion of a great deal of astronomical and other scientific data based on fuller records than Mr. Henson, in the nature of the case, was able to compile," implying Henson's inferior intellect and subordinate role in the expedition. The reviewer concludes that the text will likely be of interest to those who would "hesitate before the formidable bulk of Peary's own authoritative account," again emphasizing Henson's deficiencies in relation to Peary.[28]

Despite Peary's and reviewers' efforts to undermine Henson's status as an explorer, he embraces the exploration narrative form and ethos in various ways, particularly when he narrates his adventures as a team leader appointed by Peary. Through brutal and life-threatening conditions, Henson breaks trail for Peary (recalling the hard work that Olney describes as a trait of the slave narrative), who, Henson claims, has to make most of the journey riding in a sledge because of injuries sustained on a prior expedition. In fact, Henson writes, Peary "was practically a dead weight" but hastens to add that the reader should "not think that we could have gotten back without him, for it was due to the fact that he was with us, and that we could depend upon him to direct and order us, that we were able to keep up the break-neck pace." In deference to the white imperialist authority that sanctions and defines the expedition, Henson is careful to acknowledge Peary's continuing status as "the heart and head of the party."[29] Peary himself claims that he brings up the rear in order that, he writes, "I might have everything ahead of me and know just how things were going."[30]

I suggest that we read Henson's characterization of Peary as "heart and head of the party" as ironic. Indeed, given Henson's emphasis on his own hard work and his ability to lead, Peary becomes somewhat superfluous in Henson's account, particularly to the success of the return trip. At the same time, Henson identifies Peary's rallying cry of "Forward! March!" as that which motivates him in his own work of exploration, and he takes it upon himself to persuade others in the party to accept Peary's view of the expedition. In some instances he relinquishes his own perspective and becomes Peary's spokesman. When some of the Eskimos express concern about the danger of the expedition and want to turn back, he writes, "I have had the Devil's own time in making my boys and some of the others see it the way the Commander wants us to look at it." Similarly, when Henson builds sledges from a new pattern, he refers to Peary as the one who has "designed" them and to himself as the one who has "done the work," an appropriate metaphor for their relationship as Henson often represents it throughout the narrative. Henson suggests that they had always proceeded in this fashion. He writes that, as a young man, upon first meeting Peary, the "instinct of [his] race" allowed him to recognize qualities in Peary that made him "willing to engage . . . in his service," and that since that time, he has been a member of every Peary expedition as an "assistant"—"a term," in Henson's words, "that covers a multitude of duties, abilities, and responsibilities."[31] Henson's characterization of himself as naturally and racially inclined to assist a white man parallels the portrait of Henson in Washington's introduction as typically subordinate.

This characterization is further supported at other moments in the text as Henson receives and carries out orders from Peary. These duties often involve the most unpleasant tasks of the expedition, such as trading tin plates and cups for Eskimo sled dogs, an exchange that Henson views as dishonest: "I have known men who needed dogs less to pay a great deal more for one pup than was paid to Nipsangwah for his pack of seven." Through his characterization of Peary as a taskmaster in *A Negro Explorer*, he is also able both to critique the great explorer and to represent himself as a hardworking member of the expedition, despite hardships. During the first part of the pole journey, Henson writes that he has been so busy responding to orders of "'Matt do this' and 'Matt do that'" that he has had no time to update his diary, and later Henson notes that when Peary arrives in camp, all comfort and leisure come to an end, for "the Peary discipline is the iron hand ungloved." Peary sometimes chastises Henson and other members of the party, and after one accident in which a member of the party, Kudlooktoo, has an accident and breaks his sledge, Henson remarks, "You would have thought that Kudlooktoo was the last person in Commander Peary's estimation, when he got through talking to him and telling him what he thought of him." Henson claims that Peary also forces them to travel in conditions that no other expedition leader would attempt. He relates one instance in which they "battled all day with the wind, which had blown a full-sized gale," recalling, "Our breath was frozen to our hoods of fur and our cheeks and noses frozen," resulting in a sleepless night that Henson describes as "Plutonian Purgatory."[32] His representation of himself as industrious and hardworking through these privations, like an African American laborer toiling for a demanding white overseer, further aligns his travel narrative with the slave narrative form.

Henson's reference to his "abilities and responsibilities" as Peary's assistant, however, also calls attention to his assertion of subjectivity and expertise throughout the narrative. Henson's representation of himself as a leader recalls Equiano's representation of his seafaring expertise in his slave narrative, where he notes at one point, "Many were surprised when they heard of my conducting the sloop into the port [at Montserrat], and I now obtained a new appellation, and was called Captain."[33] Peary himself alludes to Henson's expertise in acknowledging his translation and igloo-building abilities, calling him the "best man" in his party for Arctic work.[34] Henson establishes his own credentials as a veteran Arctic explorer by referring to a young, athletic, and enthusiastic member of their party, George Borup, as "the kid," and noting that he'd anticipated Borup's departure from the expedition because he had "seen too many enthusiastic starters" who "did not finish well." Additionally, at various points in the narrative, Henson, as expert, instructs the reader in the histories and best practices of Arctic exploration, and as he recalls his previous journeys over the same ground and past familiar landmarks, he emphasizes his status as an experienced traveler and explorer. For example, as they traverse Duck Island, he recalls his time ashore there in 1891, "on my first voyage north," adding: "I remember distinctly the cairn the party built and the money they deposited in it. I wonder if it is still there?"[35] He also remarks in the *Boston American* article, which was published after the 1909 discovery, "I can see now that we could have reached the North Pole in 1906 if we had made haste in the colder season."[36] Such passages signal to the reader his experience and familiarity with the Arctic.

He demonstrates his authority through comments about the necessities required for Arctic travel, too, noting of their ship, the *Roosevelt,* that such a vessel "is the prime necessity in getting an expedition within striking distance of the Pole, but once here the ship (and no other boat but the *Roosevelt* could get here) is not indispensable, and accordingly all precautions against her loss were taken." Displaying his knowledge of Arctic history, he observes that "Arctic explorations have lost their ships early in the season and in spite of the loss have done successful work. The last Ziegler Polar Expedition of 1903–1905 is an example." But he concludes that the *Roosevelt* "is a 'Homer' and we confidently expect to have her take us back to home and loved ones." This statement reveals that he is not only experienced but also able to make predictions about the likely outcomes of Arctic travel.[37]

His various anecdotes about Arctic life and travel also establish him as a credible expert, such as his humorous advice about how to harness a dog team, with as little blood loss as possible. Sometimes, Henson represents himself as a kind of guide to his readers. For example, at the beginning of chapter 7 he directs the reader: "If you will get out your geography and turn to the map of the Western Hemisphere you will be able to follow me. Take the seventieth meridian, west . . . our pathway to the Pole."[38] Henson's language here is notable for its assertiveness. By instructing readers to take out their maps and follow him, he highlights his role as a trail breaker (particularly for Peary, as seen in his emphasis on Peary bringing up the rear), as well as a leader and an explorer in his own right, conquering geographical space and achieving significant conquests.

From such passages it is apparent that Henson views himself as a major player in the discovery of the pole. He represents himself as decisive and, because of his Arctic experience, able to react to changing conditions for the benefit of the expedition, thereby establishing and emphasizing his authority. During one segment of the trip, a member of the party, Captain Bob Bartlett, travels ahead, instructing Henson and his crew to sleep at each igloo he will build in advance; in the igloos, he leaves a note with further instructions for Henson. Yet Henson ignores these instructions from his white superior, writing, "In spite of these previous arrangements, I felt that with such good traveling it would be just as wise to keep on going, and so we did." He also reports conversations with other members of the party in which he participates as an equal and even an adviser, or as someone with superior experience and moral advice to share. For example, when team member Donald MacMillan asks Henson whether or not he should disclose an injury to Peary (which will likely terminate his journey toward the pole), Henson advises him "to make a clean breast of it." Eventually Henson and his men become the advance team for the rest of the group, a responsibility that allows him to emphasize his leadership and authority as an explorer on this segment of the journey. He writes, "My [Eskimo] boys, Ootah, Ahwatingwah, and Koolootingwah, under my command started north, to pioneer the route for five full marches, and it was with a firm resolve that I determined to cover a big mileage."[39]

Henson's use of terms such as "command," "pioneer," and "determined" (not to mention "boys") coincide with the imperialist discourse and ideology of the late nineteenth- and early twentieth-century exploration narrative, and *A Negro Explorer* is distinctive as a narrative in which a black explorer claims these terms as his own. Stephanie Leigh Batiste has investigated African American performers' "use of representational structures that sustained the imperial project" during the depression era. Although her study focuses on black performance later in the century, some of her conclusions about African Americans' investment in imperialism illuminate Henson's earlier narrative representation of this relationship. Batiste observes that sometimes African American subjectivity "developed through consent and complicity with imperial discourses and their effects," often resulting in "the articulation of more complicated formations of identity, including equality, resistance, [and] superiority." Batiste also argues that African Americans' participation in imperialist discourse reveals a "desire for national identification and inclusion," and these "imperial representations . . . act as a display of integration and assimilation."[40] Henson utilizes imperialistic rhetoric in order to assert his identity as a black explorer equal and sometimes superior to Peary and to resist representations of him and his work by Peary and others that compromise this identity. His participation with Peary in this conquest promoting the international reputation of the United States undoubtedly heightens his sense of national identification and integration, which Batiste identifies as a feature of African American imperialist discourse.

In asserting imperialist ideology through his representation of the Eskimos and his relationship to them, Henson resorts to a racial hierarchy similar to that with which he himself would have contended. He says that in his Arctic journeys, he has lived among a people who, according to the science of the day, "represented the earliest form of human life" and lived in conditions akin to "the Stone Age." In what seems to be an Arctic version of "going native," Henson claims that he reverts to the Eskimo "stage of life by leaps and bounds" and comes to love and understand the Eskimos, and they him.[41] But he also claims that he is able to switch back to a civilized way of life just as quickly as he adapts to the Eskimo's primitive state.

Henson's characterization of the primitive North contrasts with popular notions about uncivilized groups being better adapted to warmer climes. Nicolás Wey Gómez examines stereotypes of North and South in *Tropics of Empire: Why Columbus Sailed South to the Indies* (2008), showing how Columbus undertook his exploration in the context of early scientific traditions that drew connections between latitude and culture and assumed the relatively undeveloped and uncivilized nature of more southern, warmer areas of the globe in contrast to the cooler and civilized northern regions.[42] Such distinctions persisted into the early twentieth century and validated the imperial project of making European subjects of those living in the tropics. Henson himself referred to how he overcame such scientific determinism and the assumption that a black man "could not stand the cold" by surviving the Arctic conditions and returning unscathed.[43] This characterization not only challenges conventional racial categories but also, as Foy suggests, highlights African Americans' geographical and cultural mobility, despite social restrictions in the United States.[44]

Throughout Henson's narrative, however, the Eskimos—or huskies, as Henson sometimes refers to them—remain the northern primitive Other, and Henson categorizes them alongside the sled dogs in terms of interesting Arctic curiosities.[45] His representation of the Eskimos runs the gamut of popular racial stereotypes. Reverting to assumptions about the dirt and filth of the Other, often applied to immigrants in early twentieth-century American discourse,[46] Henson observes that the Eskimos who live on board the ship are "cleaner in their personal habits than they were wont to be in their own home country, but never for an instant does the order or appearance of an Esquimo's habitation suggest the rose or geranium." Henson represents Eskimos as noble savages corrupted through contact with outsiders. They are the "best-natured people on earth," he insists, "with no bad habits of their own, but a ready ability to assimilate the vices of civilization," noting that although they have adopted tobacco, "whisky has not yet gotten in its demoralizing work."[47] As Ann Fienup-Riordan points out, like Native Americans, "Eskimos were alternately depicted as Arcadians and as savages—simultaneously heroes and brutes; free of the constraints of civilization yet subject to extreme natural hardship and ordeal; idealized as healthy, vital, and noble and at the same time condemned as rude, ugly, and barbaric." She observes that accounts of Eskimos written in the late eighteenth and early nineteenth centuries illustrate this ambivalence, as do the journal accounts of Arctic explorers.[48]

Of Peary, Fienup-Riordan notes his "patronizing" depiction of Eskimos, particularly in a brief sketch in his 1898 book *Northward Over the Great Ice*, where he describes the Smith Sound Eskimos as "a community of children in their simplicity, honesty, and happy lack of all care; of animals in their surroundings, their food and habits." At the same time, Peary acknowledges their "high intelligence in the construction and use of the implements of the chase, and the ingenious concentration of every one of the few possibilities of the barren country which is their home, upon the two great problems of their existence—something to eat, and something to wear."[49] Of course, such a portrayal still plays into notions of the noble savage whose intellect does not engage with anything beyond issues of subsistence.

Fienup-Riordan states that through these accounts, "nineteenth-century Euro-Americans began to clothe the Eskimos in a new, romantic image that they wear to this day," observing the Euro-American fascination with the "sharp contrast between the harsh, cold, primordial condition of arctic life and the ultimately admirable human qualities and adaptive strengths attributed to its aboriginal occupants."[50]

Henson depicts his own adaptation to Arctic life in similarly positive terms, particularly as he narrates his hard work as a member of the expedition team, but he consistently uses the noble savage trope to describe his Eskimo team members. In Henson's text, the imagery of the noble savage merges with the trope of the vanishing native as he predicts the extinction of the small tribe with which he is acquainted. This extinction, he writes, "will be caused partly by themselves, and partly by the misguided endeavors of civilized people." He utilizes animal imagery in his description of the somewhat less than human Eskimo family: "They are very human in their attributes, and in spite of the fact that their diet is practically meat only, . . . there is a great deal of affection among them. . . . An Esquimo mother washes her baby the same way a cat washes her kittens. There are lots of personal habits the description of which might scatter the reading circle, so I will desist with the bald statement that, for them, dirt and filth have no terrors." In addition to the connections here to stereotypes of dirt and otherness, this reference to the reading circle suggests Henson's efforts to appeal to his readers' domestic cultural values and perhaps even to female readers. His description of the makeshift "circulating library" that he and his fellow team members set up to share literature also gestures toward such values and imagines the formation of a community of readers paralleling the reading circle whose sensibilities he wishes to protect.[51]

Racial stereotypes persist as well in Henson's description of his Eskimo companions' tendency to complain on the trail: "It is fierce listening to their whines and howls. Of all yellow-livered curs deliver me."[52] Such imagery reappears when Henson describes the actual discovery of the pole, as I discuss shortly, and this imagery facilitates Henson's negotiation of authority as a traveler and explorer, making his assertion of authority problematic in its reliance on cultural stereotypes. The fact that Henson would resort to such stereotypes to assert his own authority illustrates how the explorer's identity in general depended on these categories and hierarchies, and Henson's tendency to slip into similar modes of categorization when establishing his own identity as an explorer reveals the ubiquitous nature of such thinking.

Henson's depiction of the events leading up to the discovery of the pole further emphasizes his status as an explorer and the dialectic of assistant and explorer that I discussed at the beginning of the chapter. Throughout the journey Peary sends various members of the party back to the ship, and Henson is never quite sure if he might be next, suggesting that, at least from his perspective, his position in the party and in the exploration culture is far from secure. But by April 1, when Peary sends Bartlett back, Henson knows that he will get to accompany Peary to the pole. Henson writes of Bartlett, "He turned back from the Farthest North that had ever been reached by any one, to insure the safe return of him who was to go to a still Farther North, the very top of the world, the Pole itself."[53] Although we might assume that "him who was to go to . . . the Pole itself" refers to Peary, I would suggest that Henson also alludes here to his own conquest of the pole.

Once Bartlett leaves, Henson notes that an unspoken understanding passes between him and Peary: "As we looked at each other we realized our position, and we knew without speaking that the time had come for us to demonstrate that we were the men who, it had been ordained, should unlock the door which held the mystery of the Arctic." In relation to the pole discovery itself, it appeared that Peary had overshot the mark and the team had already reached the pole even as Peary continued to take navigational readings to determine its location. Henson suspected as much and mentions the fact in both *A Negro Explorer* and his 1910 *Boston American* magazine article.[54] In his 1939 interview with Lowell Thomas, Henson suggests that he reached the pole before Peary, recounting, "I calculated about how far I had come, and I said to myself, 'If I'm not on the Pole, I've crossed it, so I don't have to go no further.'" When Peary arrives, forty-five minutes behind, Henson reportedly says to him, "I think we crossed the Pole," to which Peary replies, "I guess you're right."[55] These details emphasize Henson's superior or at least equal footing with Peary in the momentous discovery.

In a 1910 article in *The World's Work,* however, Henson casts himself as Peary's "personal attendant" and expresses gratitude for "the honor of representing my race in the historic achievement."[56] In *A Negro Explorer,* Henson accepts co-credit for the discovery but describes his feelings about the event in a tellingly self-deprecating fashion:

> Another world's accomplishment was done and finished, and as in the past, from the beginning of history, wherever the world's work was done by a white man, he had been accompanied by a colored man. From the building of the pyramids and the journey to the Cross, to the discovery of the new world and the discovery of the North Pole, the Negro had been the faithful and constant companion of the Caucasian, and I felt all that it was possible for me to feel, that it was I, a lowly member of my race, who had been chosen by fate to represent it, at this, almost the last of the world's great *work.*[57]

Henson's use of terms such as "accompanied" and "faithful and constant companion of the Caucasian" emphasizes his assistant role, while at the same time, his reference to his role in "the last of the world's great *work*" underscores his significant participation in this final frontier of exploration as a representative of the black race. Henson aligns both the imperial project and world history more generally with African American accomplishment through this reference, anticipating Langston Hughes's similar (though less imperialistic) projection of African American experience onto world history in his important 1921 poem "The Negro Speaks of Rivers."[58] Like the speaker of Hughes's poem, Henson's comment suggests a shared black experience, but at the same time, his depiction of himself as "chosen by fate" for his role in the discovery highlights his individual experience and accomplishment.

Significantly, Henson suggests that it is fate, rather than his own hard work and ability, that has chosen him for this moment of discovery despite the fact that he has documented his work and ability at great length in his narrative. In contrast, he credits Peary's success to the leader's own superior initiative: "Commander Peary had taken the North Pole by conquest, in the face of almost insuperable natural difficulties, by the tremendous fighting-power of himself."[59] Henson's reference to "insuperable natural difficulties" could refer to both Peary's overcoming his physical limitations to achieve the feat (having to ride for most of the journey in a sledge because of his injured feet, according to Henson's *Boston American* article)[60] and his enduring the extreme conditions, a detail that appears in Euro-American accounts as a trait that non-natives admired in Eskimos. The notion that Peary accomplishes his feat "by the tremendous fighting-power of *himself*" seems to cast Peary as the sole Arctic conqueror and discoverer of the pole, as in the prefatory materials by Roosevelt and Grosvenor, and elides Henson's role in the accomplishment.

This perspective is also borne out in Peary's narrative of the expedition, including the photographs displayed in his book. Peary includes as a frontispiece the picture taken at the pole of Henson hoisting the polar flag, surrounded by the Eskimo members of the party (fig. 1); the only other pictures of Henson in Peary's book include him in group shots with the Eskimos. Individual photographs of U.S. members of the expedition appear, but they do not include Henson.[61] Similarly, George Borup's letter to his father about the expedition, published in the *New York Times* in 1909, contains references to Peary, Donald MacMillan, Ross Marvin, and Borup's Eskimo companion, but not to Henson.[62] Further emphasizing the discovery as Peary's individual accomplishment, Henson himself characterizes Peary as determined to conquer the Arctic frontier in the face of insurmountable obstacles and as having contributed to the storehouse of scientific knowledge, like the members of the National Geographic Society, to which Henson was never admitted during his lifetime.[63] Peary has "added to the sum of Earth's knowledge," Henson writes, "and proven that the mind of man is boundless in its desire," adding, "There is no more beyond . . . and the geographical mind is at rest."[64] In other words, Peary has closed the book on the Earth's last frontier of discovery.

Henson, however, undermines this portrayal of Peary in several ways. As I have mentioned, Peary was injured and was carried in a sledge for most of the journey. Henson writes that "Commander Peary had had the best of the going, for he had brought up the rear and had utilized the trail made by the preceding parties, and thus he had kept himself in the best condition for the time when he made the spurt that brought him to the end of the race." This image of the diminished Peary carried in a sledge, benefiting from the trail already broken for him, and saving himself for the final push at the end contrasts dramatically with the many images Henson provides of himself contending with extreme weather conditions and physical hardships in order to break a trail for Peary to follow. Furthermore, when describing the discovery of the pole, Henson alludes to Peary's mean-spiritedness. Just as Peary keeps Henson in the dark about whether or not he will be the remaining team member to accompany him to the pole, Henson claims that Peary also keeps secret the actual day of the trek to the pole. Henson writes that on April 6, 1909, he notices that Peary has pulled out of his coat "a small folded package and unfolded it." Henson "recognized his old silk flag, and realized that this was to be a camp of importance," as Henson knows that Peary always flies this flag at his last camp, though Peary has not

FIGURE 1. "The Five Flags at the Pole." Source: Robert Peary, *The North Pole* (1910).

informed Henson that this is the case. This scene is one of the few allusions in Henson's narrative to an attempt on Peary's part to exclude Henson from the final discovery.[65]

In his *Boston American* article, Henson more explicitly discusses Peary's plans to leave him in camp to avoid having to share the discovery of the pole,[66] and he describes Peary's subsequent coldness toward him and his attempts to prevent Henson from lecturing about the expedition. Some of this coldness is alluded to in *A Negro Explorer* as Henson describes Peary's demeanor after taking the last elevation reading to determine that they had reached the pole: "Feeling that the time had come, I ungloved my right hand and went forward to congratulate him on the success of our eighteen years of effort, but a gust of wind blew something into his eye, or else the burning pain caused by his prolonged look at the reflection of the limb of the sun forced him to turn aside; and with both hands covering his eyes, he gave us orders to not let him sleep for more than four hours."[67] Though it is possible that Peary really does experience problems with his eyes in this scene, the unconsummated handshake also implies Peary's reluctance to share the victory with his African American team member, a conclusion that Henson would express more strongly in the *Boston American* article.

Yet Henson seems to retract his accusations against Peary in a 1910 letter to the editor of *Hampton's Magazine,* in which he claims that any statement he "had turned against" Peary was simply "newspaper talk" and that his only criticism of Peary was his request that Henson not publish his photographs of the expedition. In the 1939 Lowell Thomas interview, Henson further remarks that he assumed Peary was angry with him for going on the lecture circuit after the expedition, but, Henson adds, "I had to make a living."[68] In the *Negro Explorer* excerpt, it is curious that Henson provides Peary with an excuse, suggesting that there may be an explanation for his actions that does not represent a slight against Henson. Perhaps Henson provides Peary with this avenue of escape because of the publication of *A Negro Explorer* in a cultural context informed by Jim Crow policies and suspicious of a black man's derogatory remarks about a well-known white explorer.[69]

But Henson's depiction of the abortive handshake at the pole also functions as another instance of the veiled critique of Peary that Henson incorporates throughout the narrative. This critique is further suggested by the fact that in *A Negro Explorer,* Henson spends less time describing

Peary's behavior at the moment of conquest than he does describing the four Eskimo men who stood with him and Peary at the pole, noting their strengths and accomplishments as hunters, fathers, and expedition members. Even as he gives credit to these Eskimo team members, he invokes the imperialistic and racist imagery that appears elsewhere in the text to assert that the four men were blindly devoted companions to Peary, and possessing the same fidelity as the dogs, "insured the success of the master."[70] As with the earlier remark that might be read as a veiled reference to himself as the one chosen to reach the pole when Barlett leaves, this too could refer to Henson as master. In contrast to the tendency of slave narrative authors to "present themselves as typical products of slavery" and thereby critique the entire system,[71] Henson takes pains to represent himself as atypical in his role as an explorer, but he does so by employing the imperialist and racist rhetoric of conquest to elevate his own stature in his text and in the larger narrative of the pole discovery.

Henson gives few details about the return trip from the pole to the ship except to note that it was a "horrid nightmare" and impossible to describe.[72] Although we might expect that the narrative of the return is less important than that of the push to the pole since the conquest is now complete, the fact that the return trip is "horrid" and unspeakable underscores both the physical and emotional toll of the journey. Richard Davis observes that the second half of exploration narratives sometimes reveals the desire to get home as quickly as possible,[73] and Henson's narrative follows this pattern. But the most painful aspect of the return trip seems to have been Peary's coldness toward Henson rather than the physical hardship of the trail. In his *Boston American* article, Henson claims that despite their many years together, he and Peary are "strangers" after the pole expedition: "From the moment I declared to Commander Peary that I believed we stood upon the Pole he apparently ceased to be my friend." Peary, he adds, "did not speak to me four times on the whole return journey to the ship. I thought this over and it grieved me much." Remembering how he had helped Peary when the commander lost his toes to frostbite and how he had foraged for food "to keep him alive," Peary's indifference to him on the return journey, Henson says, "nearly broke my heart," and he claims that Peary even refused to bid him farewell when they parted in New York.[74]

In the context of the slave narrative tradition, Henson's experience recalls the emotional distress that some authors experience in relation to indifferent or unkind treatment from masters or other individuals with whom they have built a bond. Many slave narratives are marked by heightened sentiment,[75] which, Christine Levecq argues, black writers used to engage with contemporary ideologies and "to promote . . . a particular vision of society."[76] Considering the connections between the slave narrative and the sentimental novel, Cindy Weinstein argues that when we reverse conventional lines of influence which suggest, as Hazel Carby and Karen Sánchez-Eppler do, that slave narratives both appropriate and subvert sentimental convention in order to court white sympathy, and instead view the sentimental novel through the lens of the slave narrative, we recognize how "the production of the white sentimental heroine's freedom is intimately linked with the story of the slave's bondage." That is, such novels "assure readers that the past, especially if that past has contained a descent into slavery, will never again threaten to intrude upon the present" and "to be rescued is to be rescued not only from one's past but even from remembering it."[77] Weinstein's use of the slave narrative as a critical frame for the sentimental tradition allows us to reconsider how the sentimental novel elides the emotional horrors of slavery on which its plot and characterizations depend.

Such a view coincides with recent critical work on sentiment in the neo–slave narrative.[78] Keith Byerman argues that through a sentimental view of slavery, one can be "seduced by horror either by believing that the past can be manipulated to one's own ends or by believing that the past is so powerful that one has no responsibility to the present." In a neo–slave narrative such as Toni Morrison's *Beloved,* characters demonstrate "a refusal to be paralyzed by history and an engagement in community as a means to change the present."[79] Furthermore, the aspects of slavery that the sentimental novel might elide are foregrounded in a novel like *Beloved.* As Timothy Spaulding observes, Morrison "forces readers to shift their focus away from the fantastic elements like the haunted house and the ghost toward the 'real' gothic elements of the text: slavery itself and those who systematically perpetuated it."[80] As I have argued elsewhere, the cultural work of such narratives includes an attention to the affective agency of characters, through which they construct alternative stories that challenge powerful dominant-culture narratives and empower readers to use the difficult facts of slave history to improve their present conditions and communities.[81]

While Henson's narrative is not necessarily a neo–slave narrative, it extends in new directions the emotional work of the slave narrative in challenging dominant stories. We might expect to find in Henson's narrative domestic and even filial devotion, as found in Equiano and other slave narrative authors, but because of the many years he has shared with Peary traveling together and enduring hardships, the relationship seems to exceed mere loyalty (though Peary emphasizes Henson's loyalty in his account) and approaches something more akin to professional affinity and respect. In the *Boston American,* Henson emphasizes his strong bond with Peary just before noting the ending of their friendship, a juxtaposition that heightens the effect of the separation: "Commander Peary, the employer, and I, plain Matt Henson, the servant, had worked and starved and frozen together. From the moment I declared to Commander Peary that I believed we stood upon the Pole he apparently ceased to be my friend."[82] Given the two men's shared history, which Henson exploits in his narrative to sustain his own authority, Peary's rebuff of Henson is particularly surprising and hurtful. Henson observes that once he arrives back at the ship, and during the three weeks of idleness that ensue, Peary speaks hardly a word to him and mentions nothing "about the North Pole or anything connected with it."[83] Once the ship reaches Cape Breton Island, Peary joins his wife and children on a train ride home while Henson continues home on the ship, and these separate travel routes and vehicles provide a fitting metaphor for the rift between the two explorers that persisted through the end of their lives.[84]

Henson's negotiation of emotional experience, African American identity, and travel genres informs his portrayal of the fluctuating nature of his and Peary's relationship, as well as their authority as explorers. This fluctuation reflects what we might consider, in Paul Smethurst's terms, the ways in which imperialistic narrative form imposes order on a "disorderly mobility."[85] Henson's efforts both to conform to and to subvert such orderliness results in a distinctive portrayal of black identity and mobility. The identity of the explorer that Henson examines in his narrative would not survive long after the book was published. Indeed, Davis notes that "the science of aviation, developed in support of the war effort, virtually rendered both the wilderness and the explorer . . . obsolete curiosities of an earlier age."[86] Yet the tension in Henson's narrative between the inscription and erasure of his subjectivity as a black explorer and traveler provides insights into the cultural work performed by African American travel narratives and serves as a model for how black travelers and their texts engage with the genre traits of travel literature to challenge dominant ideologies about African American experience and identity during the age of Jim Crow. Jessie Redmon Fauset further extends this exploration of genre traits and disorderly mobility, though in a much different context, in her *Crisis* travel essays from the 1920s, as I discuss in the next chapter.

4

CULTURAL WORK, DISORDERLY MOBILITY, AND THE MUNDANE REALITIES OF TRAVEL

Jessie Redmon Fauset and *The Crisis*

Unlike Matthew Henson, Jessie Redmon Fauset makes less explicit claims to the African American traveler's authority in her 1921 and 1925–26 travel essays in *The Crisis* magazine, where she was literary editor from 1919 until she left in 1926. Like Ida B. Wells and Zora Neale Hurston, Fauset invokes her black mobile body in her travel accounts, but she does so less overtly than these other black female travel writers and in the context of middle-class bourgeois values during the Harlem Renaissance.[1] The issue of respectability, in particular, arises in interesting ways in Fauset's work. For example, though she is not adverse to discussing sexuality in her novels, even if in a veiled manner, her concerns about fictional depictions of sexuality are apparent in her 1922 article, "Some Notes on Color," where she writes that while she views René Maran's *Batouala* (1922) as "a marvelous piece of artistry, . . . we are half glad it is written in French so that the average white American won't insist that here is the true African prototype."[2] Indeed, as Michel Fabre notes, "her excessive good breeding" caused her to decline the offer to translate Maran's novel, "lest his crude descriptions of African life ruin her respectability."[3] In a letter to Joel

Spingarn, she explained: "I know my own milieu too well. If I should translate that book over my name I'd never be considered 'respectable' again." Yet at the same time, Fabre contends, "she gave the impression that she would enjoy nothing more than going slumming with [Langston] Hughes around Paris."[4] Of her novels, Fauset's *Plum Bun* (1929) offers perhaps the most sustained examination of the constraints that respectability places on African American women's lives.

In her *Crisis* travel essays, Fauset situates the mundane details of life abroad within a discussion of social respectability and moral responsibility. Her emphasis on everyday realities contrasts with her less frequent discussions of class and racial oppression. Other critics have also noted both her reference to the mundane and the excellence of her essays. Cheryl A. Wall argues that "Fauset achieved more distinction as a journalist and essayist" than as a novelist and that "her personal essays contain her best writing."[5] Farah J. Griffin and Cheryl J. Fish also note the excellence of Fauset's essays and observe that she is "at her best" when describing the "ordinary" and "mundane."[6] Her essays include banalities germane to the travel narrative, such as descriptions of the local scene and customs, accommodations and food, and inconveniences. But her insertion of social questions into the travel essays contrasts with the banal details of travel and issues of respectability and highlights the oscillation between conservatism and cultural critique that informs her representation of African American mobility and identity.

Fauset has been characterized as a member of the Harlem Renaissance's "rear guard" of conventional, "imitative" writers who avoided innovative form and content in order to court white critical approval.[7] Her work has been criticized as "sentimental," "sophomoric, trivial, and dull,"[8] though she also championed black radicals such as Claude McKay. W. E. B. Du Bois, however, counted her among the young writers whose work "will mark an epoch" in black writing. According to Alain Locke, Fauset's first novel, *There Is Confusion* (1924), represents what "the Negro intelligentzia [*sic*] have been clamoring for": "a cross section of the race life higher up the social pyramid and further from the base-line of the peasant and the soil than is usually taken." He explicitly links the novel to middle-class respectability, noting that "it throbs with some of the latest reactions of the race situation in this country upon the psychology and relations of colored and white Americans of the more intelligent classes. It is this delineation of the problem as seen from the heights of respectability and from at least a plateau of culture that sharply differentiates Miss Fauset's novel from others." Furthermore, he notes that the "*confusions*" characters encounter in the book "*are those more universal ones of human nature and its type-psychologies.*"[9] In contrast to his negative reaction to what he viewed as racial stereotypes in Hurston's *Their Eyes Were Watching God* (1937), Locke praises Fauset's attempt to challenge stereotypes of the mulatto through serious social fiction.

A Boni and Liveright ad for *There Is Confusion* in the April 1924 *Crisis* similarly emphasizes the novel's status as social document fiction. The copy reads, "Describing with deep imaginative insight the life among the intellectual circles developing in northern cities among colored people, [Fauset] has given to the world the first lucid presentation of Negro cultural life, in a story that throbs with passion and drama." The ad also contains an endorsement by Locke, underscoring the novel's important social function: "It can be confidently commended to that increasing band—who will welcome its reactions in the best types and classes of colored folk—a social document of sterling and intimate character."[10] In 1934 Locke continued to argue that "Negro fiction would be infinitely poorer without the persevering and slowly maturing art of Miss Fauset, and her almost single-handed championship of upper and middle class Negro life as an important subject for fiction."[11] Though Locke criticized her style, he consistently expressed approval of her fictional depiction of middle-class black life.

Recent critics have recognized the more nuanced aspects of Fauset's writing. As Kathleen Pfeiffer notes, when we "read Fauset in the context of her contemporary intellectual culture . . . [we] see that she was neither anachronistic nor marginal, as previous critics have charged."[12] Indeed, it is important to remember the central role she played in bringing about the Harlem Renaissance. Langston Hughes wrote in his 1940 autobiography *The Big Sea* that "Jessie Fauset at the *Crisis,* Charles Johnson at *Opportunity,* and Alain Locke in Washington, were the three people who midwifed the so-called New Negro Literature into being."[13] Her support and mentorship of Hughes is especially apparent in her letters to him. On May 28, 1923, Fauset wrote to him: "Your work . . . is improving by leaps and bounds. There is a surer and more mature touch. I am still not crazy personally about your prose." On June 24, 1924, she told him: "You . . . have more promise than any American poet of my acquaintance. I rank you above Edna St. Vincent Millay." She assured him in her January 6, 1925, letter,

"You . . . have the truest poetic instinct" of any U.S. poet, black or white. In letters on October 14 and October 23, 1925, she advised him to show due consideration for Du Bois's support by dedicating a poem to him and in the later letter suggested how he might access funds to pay for college. Her respect for Hughes is reflected in her willingness to share her own writing ideas with him and to count him in her June 24, 1924, letter as one of her esteemed "younger contemporaries."[14]

Fauset championed black culture more generally in essays such as her "New Literature of the Negro" article of June 1920, in which, as Abby Arthur Johnson suggests, she "urged [black] readers to find satisfaction in their own heritage."[15] According to Claude McKay, "all the radicals liked her, although in her social viewpoint she was away over on the other side of the fence."[16] Yet her concerns about fiction that portrayed the seedier aspects of black life are confirmed by other artists' responses to the question of black representation in the *Crisis* symposium "The Negro in Art: How Shall He Be Portrayed?" Though acknowledging that writers were not obliged to portray any particular type of character, those responding to the question also claimed that the trend of depicting unsavory black figures is "a grave danger making for a literary insincerity both insidious and abominable."[17] Similarly, in her June 24, 1924, letter to Hughes, Fauset reminded him that "it is possible to be rugged without being crude," and in an earlier letter on April 14, 1922, she asked him to send a travel sketch of Mexico to *The Crisis,* noting, "It needn't be tragic, just be beautiful,"[18] signaling her aesthetic preferences.

Unlike Locke, some critics did not approve of her artistic approach. Gerald Sykes, reviewing Fauset's novel *The Chinaberry Tree* (1931), remarks:

> The book attempts to idealize [the] polite colored world in terms of the white standards that it has adopted. And here lies Miss Fauset's artistic errors. When she parades the possessions of her upper classes and when she puts her lovers through their Fauntleroy courtesies, she is not only stressing the white standards that they have adopted; she is definitely minimizing the colored blood in them. This is a decided weakness, for it steals truth and life from the book. Is not the most precious part of a Negro work of art that which is specifically Negroid, which none but a Negro could contribute?[19]

Leroi Jones (Amiri Baraka) in the 1960s similarly argued that black writers like Fauset who were affiliated with the middle-class had impeded the rise of African American literature.[20]

This critical context is important, for an emphasis on the middle-class sensibilities of Fauset's *Crisis* essays has led to the assumption that she was opposed to the progress of the race and the promotion of black literature, a point of view that eclipses the cultural critique in her writing. Indeed, we might approach the combination of conservatism and activism in Fauset's essays in terms of the "politics of respectability" that Evelyn Brooks Higginbotham identifies in the Black Baptist Church Women's Movement of the late nineteenth and early twentieth centuries. Higginbotham writes that black Baptist women during this period "emphasized manners and morals while simultaneously asserting traditional forms of protest, such as petitions, boycotts, and verbal appeals to justice." The church work that women performed influenced the formation and work of secular organizations such as the National Association of Colored Women,[21] established in 1896, which, as Carolyn Wedin Sylvander notes, "was clearly a result of Black women having been excluded from white women's organizations and activities, and of the persistent notion that the Black woman was particularly immoral,"[22] a position against which Wells had argued vociferously.

Fauset's approach to the issue of respectability may at first blush appear to be disengaged from important racial issues, and there is little discussion of petitions or boycotts in her essays. Wells's emphasis on respectability and her efforts to resist negative characterizations of the black female body seem much more explicitly connected to the challenge posed by the black women's movement to representations of black women as "immoral, child-like, and unworthy of respect or protection."[23] But a careful reading reveals the quiet yet persistent assertiveness of Fauset's approach, which aligns her more completely with Wells and other black female travel writers than we might at first assume. The contrasts she creates between the mundane details of travel and her more oblique references to social injustice produce an understated though compelling appeal to principles of equality and allow her to resist injustice directed toward herself and others.

The fact that we find Fauset's essays published alongside reports of lynchings and articles about racial violence in *The Crisis* underscores the Jim Crow contexts informing her travel writing. An example of the magazine's emphasis on the issue of racial violence published at the same time that Fauset's travel essays appeared can be seen in the January 1924 *Crisis* as a report on the activities and resolutions of the Third Pan-African Congress, held in London and attended by *Crisis* editor W. E. B. Du Bois. The resolutions include a list of "legitimate and immediate needs of the peoples of African descent," including "trial by juries of their peers under established forms of law." For black Americans, the resolutions also ask for "the suppression of lynching and mob-law, the end of caste and the recognition of full citizenship despite race and color."[24]

Also appearing in this issue is a column, "Financing the Fight against Lynching," discussing the NAACP's financing of the Dyer Bill, which mandated legal punishment for lynching; the bill passed the United States House of Representatives but was filibustered in the Senate.[25] The column attempts to garner contributions for the bill by inducing guilt in readers about the amount they might spend on leisure activities in contrast to their financial contributions to support social justice. The writer notes that if both white and black people's "hearts . . . were stirred" to donate even one-fifth of the amount that it had cost 27,000 people to attend the recent Thanksgiving Day football game in Philadelphia (at ten dollars each), millions more people could be reached with the antilynching message, which would allow the Dyer Bill to pass in Congress and "render everlasting benefit to the Negro and the country at large instead of furnishing pleasure to the few." Indeed, "does pleasure mean more to the Negro than justice?" the writer demands. "Is an afternoon's recreation of greater moment than the ending of the burning of human beings at the stake?"[26]

The article's strategy of inducing guilt in its mostly black audience for not fully supporting the antilynching effort tends to elide white responsibility for such crimes, recalling the patterns of accommodation in Booker T. Washington's statements about lynching, as I discussed in chapter 2. While the suggestion that the black community should take matters into its own hands implies the agency of black citizens, there is little discussion in the *Crisis* column about the role of white people in racial violence, except to suggest that both blacks and whites spend more money and time on leisure than they do on the cause of social justice. This column does not represent the only perspective on racial violence presented in the magazine, however—indeed *The Crisis* offers many examples of resistance to racial violence and white blame for such violence—but it does illustrate the range of thinking on the subject within the black community.[27]

Fauset's place within this range of discourse is well illustrated by the placement of her poem "Rencontre" between the two articles on the issue of racial violence. The conventionally romantic sentiments of the poem suggest Fauset's affiliation with conservative and bourgeois literary tradition:

> My heart, which beat so passionless,
> Leaped high last night when I saw you.
> Within me surged the grief of years
> And whelmed me with its endless rue.
> My heart which slept so still, so spent,
> Awoke last night—to break anew.[28]

While some of Fauset's poetry projects a more modern sensibility, it also gestures "toward a vague universalism" and often contains "forgettable lyrics," as Wall observes.[29] Fauset seems to be referring to her more conventional poetic approach in her June 24, 1924, letter to Hughes, in which she states, "I still do not care very much for your vers libre . . . [which] is too free."[30] Because of the generalizations and sentiment in her poetry and other works, critics such as Wall view Fauset's approach, particularly in her criticism, as non-ideological, "despite the polemical aims of *The Crisis.*" Wall suggests that Fauset viewed art as serving "a moral and spiritual purpose, not a narrowly political one," and argues that the "more progressive issues that Fauset explored in her essays are relegated to subplots" in her novels or "eclipsed by her reliance on convention."[31] By contrast, Deborah E. McDowell contends that Fauset uses convention deliberately as a "deflecting mask for her more challenging concerns,"[32] a position that allows us to view the insertion of "Rencontre" between two articles related to the eradication of racial violence as an apt representation of the conventional and radical impulses simultaneously appearing in Fauset's work.

The dialectic between discourses of conservatism and political action in African American culture in general is evident in other ways in the placement and content of writing other than Fauset's in *The Crisis.* Sylvander notes that the magazine took an important stand against opinions and images that promoted black stereotypes and was "a source of information and of radical opinion on the issue of race in America." Du Bois filled the pages with both information (as in a newspaper) and culture (as in a magazine), and specifically targeted a black audience, something about which he disagreed with the NAACP board of directors.[33] For example, Charles Johnson argued in the January 1928 issue of the *Journal of Negro History* that "the more direct the appeals to Negroes, the less the support from that necessary outside group of subscribers and contributors," though, as Sylvander observes, Du Bois "managed to develop Black reader support and maintain with difficulty the 'outside' support of the white founders of the NAACP" with Fauset's assistance.[34]

At the same time, conservative discourses are represented in the magazine through, for example, a column such as "The Horizon" in the January 1924 issue remarking on the fashionable wedding of Mae Robinson, granddaughter of the late cosmetics magnate Madame C. J. Walker.[35] Immediately preceding this column are more political pieces in Fauset's "Looking Glass" column, which routinely included writing by Fauset as well as news reprinted from other sources (a tactic that Wells also employed in her writings, as noted in chapter 1). Teresa Zackodnik notes that Fauset's practice of reprinting was not only a common journalistic practice at the time but also "can be understood as recirculation in a black feminist tradition." Indeed, Zackodnik argues, "'The Looking Glass' was not the unified single voice of its author on various subjects, but was a multivoiced collage that could effectively produce other politicized, critical, and conscious readers of the press as the column proved Fauset herself was."[36] The connections in "The Horizon" between fashion, physical appearance, and femininity form the basis of Walker's beauty business empire and stand in striking contrast to a more polemical section in the "Looking Glass" article noting the Ku Klux Klan's resistance to efforts to remove "white male" as a phrase limiting the vote in the Ohio state constitution.[37] This "dissonant juxtaposition," to use Zackodnik's term,[38] within the "Looking Glass" column and across other columns and articles was typical of the magazine and reflects a similar dissonance in Fauset's travel essays.

The tension between conservative and radical impulses both in Fauset's work and in other *Crisis* articles—what we might view as an oscillation between a passive versus an active stance toward racial oppression—invokes the dialectic between stasis and mobility which Stephen Greenblatt identifies as a feature of the cultural work that texts perform,[39] and which Hurston also exploits in her travels in the Caribbean, as I discuss in chapter 5. This dialectic coincides with the ways in which cultural progress is supported or constrained in narratives about mobility, such as travel narratives. Du Bois captures this dialectic in a section of his *Crisis* opinion column in September 1924 where he states: "I do not travel. I sit very still with half-closed eyes. There is at first silence and then the roar of the world." When his acquaintances remark, "You have been away," he answers, "No, Away has been with me."[40] His comments emphasize the importance of stillness and mental reflection in the outwardly mobile travel experience.

Fauset, too, invokes this tension between the static and the mobile. By inserting critiques of racial oppression in otherwise conventional discussions about the banalities of travel, she juxtaposes this conventionality (which we might view as passive and static) with the cultural work of her writing (which we might view as active and mobile). This dichotomy is related to the tensions between form and content in early twentieth-century black writing. Sylvander explains that throughout the 1920s, "an unfamiliarity with literary form and a lack of longstanding concern with matters of form proved to be technical handicaps to the Black writer" attempting to "translat[e] experience and history into effective literary form."[41] In attempting to represent African American experience adequately in fiction, some black writers resorted to exoticism, which exposed them to additional challenges, as Sterling Brown observed: "The more truthfully we write about ourselves, the more limited our market becomes. . . . When we cease to be exotic, we do not sell well."[42] Of Fauset specifically, Sylvander argues that "in parts of her novels, [she] was quite successful in reconciling the form-content difficulty; in other parts she overwrote or preached." Sylvander notes that Fauset, like other black writers, utilized disguised forms to protest and discuss controversial topics (some of the forms Sylvander lists are the spiritual, the folktale, jazz, blues, and women's novels), deliberately concealing her critique in her work.[43] The oscillation in her travel writing between conservative and activist stances represents another important strategy through which she engages in cultural critique.

Before I more thoroughly analyze the cultural work of travel in Fauset's essays, I want to examine how the connections between cultural work and travel are present in other *Crisis* essays written during this time. A two-part essay by Clara G. Stillman in the January and February 1924 issues provides a striking illustration of how an emphasis on cultural work might appear in a piece couched as a travel narrative. The title, "A Tourist in Florida," implies that the article is a leisure-class travel account, but the photos of Daytona Normal and Industrial Institute accompanying the article point toward a different objective, and indeed, after the first few paragraphs of the first installment, Stillman's broader cultural argument appears. This installment begins as a fairly typical tourist narrative containing images and language suggesting the leisure and passivity associated with the tourist: "The first time I went South I lay for months on a porch in an open pine grove near a small lake, seeing and hearing only what came my way. Sunshine streamed about me, dancing prismatically among the long, green needles, sparkling on the water and cloud castles, irradiating the air with a soft, brilliant, clarity. This sun-drenched air, I thought, was like no other I had known. It was suave, languorous and light, gentle and gay as a caress. It made one feel tender and close to all creation. It was the soul of Florida." In addition to utilizing language and images typically found in tourist narratives, Stillman also adopts the tourist's point of view to categorize the object of her gaze stereotypically, declaring that the lazy sun-drenched atmosphere represents "the soul of Florida."[44]

In the next paragraph, Stillman sustains this tourist narrative by emphasizing the visual spectacle of local citizens. She writes: "A Negro passed through the clearing. He was tall, thin and black. He walked slowly and stiffly, looking straight ahead. Sweat glistened on his cheek bones; his skin received the sun with jet-like glitter." Stillman contrasts the leisure of tourism with the everyday realities of labor through her reference to the sound of "Negro workmen laying a street into the wilderness," but she notes that despite the noise of the workers, she "lay drowzing [*sic*] in a harmony of sun and sound, with that dark, silent figure [of the passing man] a barely perceived undertone." She casts the entire city in a leisurely light, describing Daytona as "a resort with an atmosphere of perpetual holiday. Amusement was the main business of life."[45]

The tourist narrative is irrevocably disrupted, however, when she identifies "shadows," in this "holiday world [where] Negroes did all the work," that "hovered, in the main, on the edge of the sunlit area, but sometimes they fell across one's path with a disconcerting chill." She notices that in the city's resort-like atmosphere, African Americans are made to sit in the rear of streetcars, and she sees Jim Crow notices "proclaim[ing] the division between us." She observes other evidence of racial division, noting, "Theoretically it was not new to me. But those first impressions of the actuality of the segregation were as sharp and shocking as if I had never heard of its existence." Later, when she is introduced to "life on the other side of the veil" (white society) as a visitor in various homes and institutions, she comes away from these interactions "enriched like a traveler in a strange land who feels the charm of physical and social differentness, and thrills to the still greater discovery of spiritual likeness inhabiting this difference."[46] Stillman's depiction of this cultural experience as a form of travel into strange territory heightens the sense of contrast between the resort-like atmosphere of visiting Florida and the segregated conditions of African Americans living in the region.

The remainder of the January installment of Stillman's article and all of the February installment focuses on her impressions of racial uplift efforts in the state's high schools, specifically the Florida Normal and Industrial Institute at Daytona, which offers both vocational training and college preparation. She emphasizes the school's Taylorized routine and work ethic, recalling Washington's emphasis on his own industriousness (for example, his autobiographical account of cleaning the schoolroom to gain entrance to Hampton Institute) and that of his students established by the routine and training at Tuskegee as a marker of self-worth and respectability. Stillman emphasizes the facts about the school's routine that challenge racist assumptions or lies. She writes that at Daytona "the day begins with a rising bell at 5:30 and proceeds systematically to the 'lights out' bell at 9 o'clock for students, at 10 for teachers and nurses. This is the sobering reality, giving the lie to current legends of shiftlessness and unreliability. Unfortunately, many people hear the legends. Few see the facts."[47] The reference to the rigid schedule supports her argument about the respectability of African American students and blacks in general, but it also emphasizes the ways in which the bodies and lives of these students are regulated by the mechanized routine of both institutionalized education and racism.

The implication here is that there may be a price to pay for proof of respectability. The very things that Stillman wants—education and respectability—enforce a bodily and mental rigidity made necessary by the need to marshal evidence to counter racist ideologies. She says that she has been assured that "interracial relations improve" in the vicinity of such schools and concludes that "if the white race is capable of rising to an impartial recognition of merit, here is its chance," clearly placing responsibility on the dominant culture to improve racial relations. Though she returns at the conclusion of her second installment to the opening images of the tourist narrative, the cultural significance of what she has seen and experienced in Daytona eclipses the tourist scene: "And now, when I think of Florida, my earliest impression often returns to me:—Brilliant sunshine, laughing dark figures at work; a silent, dark figure standing alone—a note of warning, not understood."[48] Racial oppression has its consequences, Stillman concludes, and as I will show, Fauset's travel writing also contains this note of warning inserted within her discussion of the travel experience.

Additional context for Fauset's treatment of black travel is provided by Claude McKay's serialized *Crisis* article "Soviet Russia and the Negro." In the concluding installment in January 1924, McKay notes the race prejudice of both the Germans and the English, somewhat in contrast to the comments of Fauset and Wells regarding the significant level of respect and freedom of mobility that they enjoy in Europe. Of his experience in Petrograd and Moscow, however, McKay observes: "I could not detect a trace of this ignorant snobbishness among the educated classes, and the attitude of the common workers, the soldiers and sailors was still more remarkable. It was so beautifully naïve; for them I was only a black member of the world of humanity." When he attends gatherings of the intelligentsia, he is invited to speak and read his poetry "and treated with every courtesy and consideration as a writer." There is "no vulgar wonderment and bounderish superiority over a Negro's being a poet,"[49] he observes, an interesting foreshadowing of Countee Cullen's poem "Yet Do I Marvel" (1925), in which the speaker notes the "curious thing: / To make a poet black, and bid him sing!"[50]

McKay, like Du Bois and Fauset, uses his interactions with these workers to argue for social justice and to resist racial oppression. Women workers in Moscow ask McKay to describe the working conditions of African American women. After hearing his description, he writes, they "passed a resolution sending greetings to the colored women workers of America, exhorting them to organize their forces and send a woman representative to Russia." Unlike Washington's descriptions, which emphasize the positive working conditions of laborers in the southern United States in relation to those abroad, McKay's article insists on the importance of southern women workers' banding together and demanding rights. Indeed, McKay calls for a spirit of revolt and agitation for civil rights among the workers of the world and suggests that one might naturally consider African Americans as sympathetic to such a spirit: "The intellectual Communists and the intelligentzia [*sic*] were interested to know that America had produced a formidable body of Negro intelligentzia and professionals, possessing a distinctive literature and cultural and business interests alien to the white man's. And they think naturally that the militant leaders of the intelligentzia must feel and express the spirit of revolt that is slumbering in the inarticulate Negro masses, precisely as the emancipation movement of the Russian masses had passed through similar phases." Here the spirit of revolt is represented as an expected consequence of the desire to be free from oppression, something to which African Americans can naturally relate. But McKay also encounters in Russia "American anti-Negro propaganda" in the comments of a female correspondent for a Danish newspaper, who states that he "should not be taken as a representative Negro for she had lived in America and found all Negroes lazy, bad and vicious, a terror to white women."[51] This same argument is used against Wells and others to counter their resistance to white power. That such sentiments parallel those that Wells encountered in the late nineteenth century underscores the lack of progress in black civil rights from the 1890s until the 1920s.

Du Bois's *Crisis* opinion pieces and sketches about his trip to Liberia are less concerned with the politics of black travel but still reveal how tourism and cultural work intermingle in the black travel text. His pieces also provide interesting contrasts with Stillman's essay. The "Opinion of W. E. B. Du Bois" for April 1924 contains journal entries typical of what one might expect from a travel diary: descriptions of natural scenes, food, accommodations, and mode of travel (in this case an ocean steamer). As in Stillman's essay, the passages are rife with reference to the leisure travel experience, noting the "languorous days," "the sea-slipping lazily south," and opportunities to "linger at the [dining] table." Du Bois's first vivid impressions of Africa emphasize the natural and cultural spectacle. He describes in a lengthy entry from New Year's Day 1924 his experience as special minister and envoy at the inauguration of the president of Liberia, claiming that this is the most significant day of his life. He remarks the important "gesture" of sending "an American Negro to Liberia" as "Envoy Extraordinary and Minister Plenipotentiary—the highest rank ever given by any country to a diplomatic agent in black Africa" and an "epochal" event.[52] He was appointed to the post by Calvin Coolidge, and a letter informing Du Bois of his appointment along with a cablegram sent to the Liberian president, Charles D. B. King, confirming Du Bois's appointment are reprinted in the "Opinion" section of the March 1924 issue of *The Crisis*.[53] Du Bois notes the "great and significant action" of "charging the envoy with a personal word of encouragement and moral support" to a newly inaugurated black president.[54] Overall, however, the entry is more generally descriptive of the events that took place than focused on the specific cultural implications of the experience.

Du Bois's "Little Portraits of Africa" in the April 1924 issue of *The Crisis* contains further entries about his time in Africa, which are even more impressionistic and sensual. In one section, subtitled "Sunday, January 13, 1924," Du Bois writes:

> Nothing is more beautiful than an African village—its harmonious colorings—its cleanliness, its dainty houses with the kitchen palaver place of entertainment, its careful delicate decorations and then the people. I believe that the African form in color and curve is the beautifulest thing on earth; the face is not so lovely—though often comely with perfect teeth and shining eyes—but the form of the slim limbs, the muscled torso, the deep full breasts!
>
> The bush is silence. Silence of things to be, silence vocal with infinite minor music and flutter and tremble—but silence, deep silence of the great void of Africa.

As in other passages in Du Bois's travel narratives, both the natural and human beauties of Africa are emphasized here, while the reference to the "void" of Africa is a curious parallel to imperialistic representations of Africa as a blank space on a map.

At the end of the piece, Du Bois sustains his exotic portrait of Africa, in contrast to its "taming" or modernization:

> The spell of Africa is upon me. The ancient witchery of her medicine is burning my drowsy, dreamy blood. . . . Africa is the Spiritual Frontier of human kind—oh the wild and beautiful adventures of its taming! But oh! the cost thereof—the endless, endless cost [of turning it into a modernized society]. Then will come a day . . . when there will spring in Africa a civilization without coal, without noise, where machinery will sing and never rush and roar, and where men will sleep and think and dance and lie prone before the rising sons, and women will be happy.

Du Bois looks forward to the time when the iron routine of labor will have ceased to exist: "The objects of life will be revolutionized. Our duty will not consist in getting up at seven, working furiously for six, ten and twelve hours, eating in sullen ravenousness or extraordinary repletion. No—We shall dream the day away and in cool dawns, in little swift hours, do all our work." In the essay Du Bois mingles travel impressions with the political and cultural work of travel and uses his romanticized vision of what Africa is and could remain to argue against its "taming."[55] Interestingly, the same iron routine that Stillman uses in her essay to argue for black strength Du Bois uses to argue for civil rights and the freedom to indulge in leisure activities, that is, to achieve the ability to fully embrace something similar to the tourist experience.

Du Bois's writing about Africa in the June 1924 *Crisis* is more overtly focused on political and cultural issues. He writes of the challenges of "pioneering" in Liberia and provides sociological observations of African manners and family life. He critiques culture in the United States, noting that it has occurred to him, when "see[ing] the awkward and ignorant missionaries sometimes sent to teach the heathen, that it would be an excellent thing if a few natives could be sent here [to the United States] to teach manners to black and white."[56] Du Bois focuses on the African individual, but not in the sensual or exoticized manner in which Stillman portrays the glistening black body or even in the same way that Du Bois himself depicts the sensual African body in his other travel pieces, as we have seen. In contrast to Wells, who actively deploys the black female body to enact cultural work, when Du Bois and Stillman turn their attention away from the spectacle of black bodies, they are able to focus more clearly on the cultural work of travel.

Fauset's travel writing in *The Crisis* reveals some of the same characteristics, including the tendency to exoticize black bodies. The cultural work of travel appears in her writing by way of her discussion about racial, class, or gender oppression, issues that are emphasized by their contrast to the banalities of travel.[57] To understand Fauset's narrative strategy and contribution to black travel writing, Paul Smethurst's argument about travel writing form and its relationship to empire proves helpful. Smethurst claims that the order imposed by imperialist ideologies and narrative forms can be disrupted by an attention to the disorderly aspects of mobility (elided in imperialist texts). We might think of the contrast in Fauset's travel essays between cultural critique and conventional travel experience as an oscillation between orderly and disorderly mobility. Smethurst associates orderly mobility with the conventions of imperialistic literary form found in "the type of narrative voice the travel writer chooses, as well as in the textual and figurative structure, and in the motifs, images, and metaphors that circulate in the text." He notes that "instability and potential disorder are necessarily suppressed within the knowledge structures that give *form* to imperialist discourse. Mobility is in conflict with imperialism's paradigms of order and control, and yet disorderly mobility is inherent in the idea of travel." Smethurst theorizes that "if we were somehow able to reinstall a proper sense of mobility, and use this against the imposed imperial (and narrative) form in European travel writing, it might help to deconstruct that form," and indeed, he points out the foregrounding of disorderly mobility that occurs in postimperial and postcolonial travel writing. Smethurst's ideas coincide with

Edward Said's arguments about the uneven exchange that exists between discourses of Orientalism and various forms of power, including the political, cultural, and moral.[58] Both Said and Smethurst encourage us to look for moments in travel texts when this unevenness is foregrounded.

In Fauset's *Crisis* essays, the contrast between mundane details and social issues brings this unevenness into view. Writing of France in "Yarrow Revisited," for example, she eloquently describes the lack of heating in her French *pension* and the lengths to which landlords will go to avoid providing it. Such commentary contrasts dramatically with the conditions of the poor on which she reflects in essays such as "Dark Algiers and White" or "This Way to the Flea Market." Indeed, Sylvander rightly notes that Fauset's travel essays "reveal a sensitivity to lives of the poor and of women, and a curiosity about ways of life other than her own,"[59] though this is a more subtle feature of her writing. Hughes provides similar details about the oppressed in his 1926 *Crisis* essay "The Fascination of Cities,"[60] but he emphasizes the romance of travel rather than the everyday, so that when he describes racial oppression, the contrast is perhaps not as stark as what we find in Fauset's essays, and thus in some ways not as effective. Indeed, Fauset's observation in "Yarrow Revisited" that in France she can take her meals in whatever tearoom "*takes [her] fancy,*"[61] alluding to the lack of such freedom in Jim Crow America and emphasizing her increased mobility in Europe, provides a stark contrast with her discussion of heating in her *pension* and reveals the ways in which the mundane experiences of travel abroad and their formal depiction in travel texts highlight issues of cultural power, identity, and mobility in African American travel writing.

Threats to black mobility and identity are clearly addressed in *Crisis* editorials such as "The Great American Specialty: Lynchings of 1923," discussing alleged offenses for, locations of, and types of lynchings. Significantly, it ends with the sentence "European papers please copy,"[62] emphasizing not only the international reach of the magazine but also the impetus, as revealed in Wells's work, to tell the lynching story outside the United States, particularly in Europe, and suggesting the difficulty of getting the antilynching message heard in the United States. While Fauset does not explicitly carry the antilynching message to Europe during her travels, she resists racial violence in subtle but effective ways. Of lynching, she writes in her 1922 article "Some Notes on Color" from *The World Tomorrow* of feeling "only the reflex of those things [beating or lynching]. Perhaps it is mere nervousness, perhaps it is something more justifiable. Often when I am sitting in a crowded assembly I think, 'I wish I had taken a seat near the door. If there should be an accident, a fire, none of these men here would help me.' "[63] The implied threat Fauset feels and describes in these situations is in some ways more effective than an outright argument against lynching and, as in Wells's essays, personalizes the threat.

Fauset is not always so effective, however, in addressing racial issues or cultural difference. In 1921 she attended the Second Pan-African Congress in London, Brussels, and Paris as a delegate of Delta Sigma Theta sorority,[64] and she wrote "Impressions of the Second Pan-African Congress" for *The Crisis* in November 1921. During her 1921 European trip, Fauset gave speeches on African American women's issues, a report of which she reprinted from the *Glasgow Herald* in her December 1921 *Crisis* article; the *Glasgow Herald* notes that "Miss Fauset . . . spoke on the subject of the colored women in America, who, she said, had been a great moving force behind all the movements for emancipation."[65] In Brussels, Fauset showed pictures of black college graduates and the first women PhDs, emphasizing her interest in education.[66] Wall notes that in the essay, Fauset tries "to convey the flavor" of the cities she visits "while reminding her readers that the wealth and the children of Africa had made much of the Old World charm possible." But as Wall contends, she drew "broad parallels between the problems of colonialism in Africa and segregation in the United States . . . [and] reflect[ed] the false simplicity of those parallels when she expressed dissatisfaction with the lack of militancy of the part of some African delegates." Of Fauset's comment "Was it that we had learned more quickly and better than they the value of organization, of frankness, of freedom of speech?" Wall observes that it "is fraught with an arrogance as terrible as it is naïve."[67]

We see this arrogance and naïveté tempered somewhat in later essays and replaced by a more sophisticated and nuanced approach to cultural issues. Fauset traveled to Europe and Africa in 1924–25 for study at the Sorbonne and the Alliance Française, and she begins several of these later travel essays by invoking memory as a stylistic device to compare and contrast her earlier impressions with her current ones. While we might assume that framing the essays by way of nostalgic memories would imbue the pieces with a romantic or even sentimental sensibility, the device actually downplays the romantic qualities of her impressions and allows her to focus on the social issues at hand. Indeed, Fauset's general approach to the subject of nostalgia is unsentimental, as poignantly explored in her August 1921 *Crisis* essay "Nostalgia." After describing in the first part of the essay the romantic longings for home in the experiences of people she meets from Greece and Italy, Fauset relates the experience of a young African American serviceman who has been serving overseas. When Fauset asks him if he is glad to be home, his response reveals his difficulty in defining "home": "Is it where one is surrounded by the sights and sounds to which he's been used all his life? Or is it where mentally and spiritually he is recognized and taken for what he is?" He tells her that he had not been back in the United States very long before he was stopped in the street by white boys exclaiming, "Nigger, you can't stay around here in that uniform." Though "born and bred in America," he was "homesick for France," where the people and customs "know how to make a man feel he's a man." Fauset observes that the black lieutenant, like all African Americans, "is doomed to know homesickness of both body and spirit. In France he will want the comforts of America; in America, he cries out for the rights of man which he knew in France," a comparison that recalls Fauset's own experience of being able to enjoy taking tea whenever and wherever she likes while in France.[68]

The theme of nostalgia in this essay and in her other travel narratives supports her cultural commentary on race relations. When she refers to her memories, the earlier impressions are often more nostalgic and touristic and tend to emphasize, by contrast, both the mundane details and the starker racial realities of her later trips. In "Yarrow Revisited," for instance, she remembers the Paris of her student days, and even the Paris of the Second Pan-African Congress only three years earlier, as "an enchanted city of gay streets, blue skies, of romantically historic monuments, a playground, a court of justice of the world . . . [in which] there was a delicious sense of *laisser-aller.*" Although she is glad for her "golden memories" of previous trips to France, she says she is "glad to be here now in this workaday season" when she can know " 'life as she is' . . . even if it is different to the verge of disappointment from preconceived notions. Truth is best. Yet dreams are fine stuff too." She takes the title of this essay from Wordsworth's trio of poems about Yarrow Water in Scotland—"Unvisited," "Visited," and "Revisited." From the last she quotes these lines: "The visions of the past / Sustain the heart in feeling / Life as she is—"; and she asserts that it is because of her past "visions" that she is "eager to know life, French life, 'as she is'" rather than dwell on romantic memories. In this regard, she acknowledges that just as the weather in Paris is not always pleasant, "so French living is not always a thing of joy and laughter,"[69] a phrase that provides a fitting segue into her discussion of the mundane.

She describes how on this visit her physical location within the city makes for a less touristic experience. Unlike on previous trips, she is not staying near the "gay, wide boulevards" or in the Latin Quarter, both of which provided her with "faulty impressions" of the real life of France. This time she is in a "small, quiet hotel . . . in the heart of a teeming business and residential section." Though she admits to loving "comfort" and "ease," she has "mapped out" a plan for herself to make the travel meaningful and instructive: time in a cheap *pension* ("Already over, thank God!" she remarks), a month in her current small hotel, a month with a French family, a month in a first-class *pension,* and additional travel as time and money permit. The cheap *pension* is terribly dreary but initially romantic. The romance wears off when she finds that the sun never penetrates to the sheltered and damp courtyard. "I'd have handed over the birthrights of all my friends and relations for an ordinary gas heater with fixtures," she claims. She spends a good deal of time in the essay complaining about and describing the French attitude toward heating, noting that the managers express surprise at her desire for a fire and give her no clear indication of when the heat will be turned on but rather put off her requests and questions with promises that it will certainly be just a "few days" more. The dreariness of her surroundings is echoed in the shabby décor and furnishings, the desiccated pensioners, and the "nondescript" food." She complains that "life in the pension is not French life only; it is life everywhere in similar environment. Only I had not thought of finding it in France,"[70] suggesting how the romantic luster of France fades in the common light of ordinary life.

Her description of the neighborhood also emphasizes the mundane details of everyday life in France. She notes the curiously broad assortment of businesses "jumbled close side by side," revealing the "hard common sense of the French which says: 'One has to have all these things in order to live; why not have them all close at hand?'" She concludes that this "decidedly logical hard matter-of-factness" is the "Frenchiest quality about the French" and speculates that if camels were to be sold, they would be crowded into this shopping district, "tethered a bit too near perhaps to the exposed cheeses and the cuts of meat," giving the suggestion of squalor, which she seems to suggest is also typical of French life. She observes that this French matter-of-factness is also evident in "the spectacle of the irreproachably dressed householder emerging from the bakery with a large half loaf of bread tucked unwrapped under his arm and that other different spectacle of the exposure of the human form upon the French stage to a degree totally unparalleled by any theatre in America." This reveals to Fauset that, for the French, life is both "bread" and "shining flesh," so "why bother to wrap up the one or to disguise the other?"[71]—references that invoke Fauset's rhetoric of respectability and the potential offense to her sensibilities that such a cultural ideal presents. Indeed, she implies that the dirt of the marketplace in which one might find camels sold alongside foodstuffs extends to the moral fiber of the country.

Some of her experiences in France counter these generalizations about lax French morals, however, and cause her to reflect on African American culture. In this teeming business district, Fauset notes that the idea of Paris as the "play-ground of the world" is contradicted, for she has "never seen people work so hard in [her] life, nor with such seriousness." She notices that the concierge in the hotel "trudges" up and down the stairs all day with heavy loads, and while there is nothing "servile" in his demeanor or actions, she can "not remember seeing any one so consciously a servant." The scene reminds her of Du Bois's notion that there is "something in colored Americans which simply will not let them work too long or too hard. That has been God's greatest gift."[72] She challenges stereotypes about the indolence of African Americans, viewing the ability to appreciate leisure as a positive quality. Like Du Bois's emphasis on Africans' right to leisure, this image counters Stillman's insistence on a rigid routine as evidence of respectability while not going as far as Du Bois toward an embrace of leisure as a cultural value. In Fauset's representation of the issue, a balance between work and leisure seems to be her ideal.

These comments, representative of the cultural work that she undertakes in her travel writing, set up the essay's conclusion, in which she reveals how the liberty she experiences in Paris is an exception to life elsewhere in the civilized world. She writes: "In Paris I find myself more American than I ever feel in America. I am more conscious of national characteristics than I have ever been in New York." This contrasts with the lack of national feeling she experiences at the Second Pan-African Congress in 1921, where she feels a more universal sense of "common blood" with other Africans.[73]

In "Yarrow Revisited" she is careful to point out that she is talking not about black American culture but about American culture in general. She observes that the public buildings in Paris bear the words "Liberté, Egalité, Fraternité," symbolizing her freedom to take her tea "*at the first tea room which takes [her] fancy.* This [liberty] is also something to be considered in reviewing French 'life as she is.' "[74]

Significantly, Fauset leaves what might arguably be her strongest and most controversial point to the very end of the essay. And it is a point that resonates with Wells's remarks about how much more freedom of mobility she experiences abroad than in the United States. Indeed, Fauset noted in a January 6, 1925, letter to Langston Hughes that in Paris it is "lovely just being oneself and not bothering about color or prejudice." In an interview published in the *Paris Herald Tribune* on February 1, 1923, she similarly remarks, "I like Paris because I find something here, something of integrity, which I seem to have strangely lost in my own country," declaring, "I like to live among people and surroundings where I am not always conscious of 'thou shall not.' "[75] She also wrote to Arthur Spingarn from Venice, "[This is] the first time since I was seventeen that I have been—comparatively—free from fetters."[76] In her travel essays, Fauset couches this message within references not to her work (as Wells does) but to the mundane realities and workaday lives of the French among whom she lives.

Fauset's impression of increased freedom in Europe is similar to that of other black travelers, such as James Weldon Johnson, who said of his first trip to Europe in 1905: "The day I set foot in France . . . I recaptured for the first time since childhood the sense of being just a human being. . . . I was suddenly free; free from a sense of impending discomfort, insecurity, danger; free from the conflict within the Man-Negro dualism and the innumerable maneuvers in thought and behavior that it compels; . . . free from special scorn, special tolerance, special condescension, special commiseration, free to be merely a man."[77] Johnson's reference to the sense of insecurity or danger parallels the nervousness Fauset expresses in "Some Notes on Color" about using public transportation. Both Johnson's and Fauset's comments about these experiences in Europe are less pointed than Du Bois's remarks in *Darkwater* (1920) about his return to the United States after two years abroad: "I builded great castles in Spain and lived therein. I dreamed and loved and wandered and sang; then, after two long years, I dropped suddenly back into 'nigger'-hating America!"[78] Indeed, while

Fauset engages in cultural commentary, she is not polemical. She hopes to ferret out the essence of French life as it is by living among the common French people, and in the process, she comments about how these experiences affect her as an African American woman abroad. Her more conservative approach is exemplified by her remarks about the unwrapped bread and scantily clad people on the stage while she simultaneously critiques racism in the United States.

Her production of cultural critique in the context of the mundane is also evident in her February 1925 essay "This Way to the Flea Market," presented as another sketch about everyday life in France. When a friend suggests to her that she should visit the Marché aux Puces, a local flea market, Fauset characterizes herself as the easily duped foreigner, likely to be preyed upon by the merchants and requiring a local guide, her friend's father, to help her through the experience. Fauset appreciates that her guide knows his neighborhood well and takes her to ordinary locations, such as a bank and a school for impoverished children, where she notes with surprise and approval that the instruction is free and a free lunch is served. The fact that she provides insights into France's social programs but does so on the way to acting as a tourist at a flea market reflects her narrative strategy of combining tourist details with cultural commentary.

The flea market itself represents both culture and tourism and, as a marketplace, emphasizes the commodified nature of the modern travel experience. But even as she navigates this touristic terrain, Fauset engages in cultural work through her observations. When she reaches the flea market, she is struck by its ordinary appearance, which reminds her of similar markets on New York's East Side. But she also notes that "not even in a big department store do I remember such a variety of objects." The abundance of items causes her to consider the excesses of modern life, the type of philosophical reflection that one commonly finds in travel narratives. She writes, "Often as I gaze around the interior of a large shop catering as modern stores do to an appreciable portion of the increasing number of our needs, I wonder what Adam and Eve would think if they might spy just once the first aids to living which civilization has gathered about itself." Here she suggests notions of respectability by eschewing modern excess in favor of her preference for the Edenic simplicity of the biblical Adam and Eve. She has the same thought at the flea market and claims that her "pen wearies" of enumerating the market's wares: "dolls, raincoats, shoe-blacking, underwear, perfumes, oil-paintings, rugs, blankets, vases, china, shoes, bicycles, old suits of clothes, hats, fans, candle-sticks, discarded curtain fixtures, table-mats, telephone boxes, cutlery, old-time firing pieces, swords, poniards, daggers, canes, rabbit-skins."[79] The long list emphasizes the accumulation of consumer goods against which she seeks a more ascetic simplicity.

The goods also provide an opportunity for cultural commentary when she observes that those who would even consider purchasing and wearing articles from the "piles of worn and faded and altogether horrible clothing" represent the poor of Europe, who "approach in the candor and simplicity of their idea of living the Adam and Eve of my conjecture. Life, the mere business of living, is their supreme occupation, let its trappings be as sordid, as infected, as repellant as may be; so long as the precious jewel of life is contained therein, what matter?" Fauset romanticizes the poor in these passages; indeed, their own Edenic simplicity, squalor, and attendant philosophy ("born of terrific experiences, not a mere dumb, driven acquiescence of the inequalities of life") might have been ripped from the pages of a Hugo novel. Yet in its contrast to the mundane commodification of the flea market, her treatment of class difference stands out. Furthermore, she refers to the haggling at the market as "a great game," and in this context her description of one female merchant who will not budge on her price for a table mat is a successful representation of French folklife. The woman's unyielding stance leads Fauset to declare:

> Her attitude, her calmness, her determination even to the point of grimness is characteristic of this class. There is something tremendously hard and stratified in the French character, a granite-like quality which results from this continuous necessity of being at grips with life itself[,] . . . the struggle for existence, the struggle with the soil and the struggle to keep the soil. And this struggle with its resulting hardness shows nowhere more plainly than in the poor and middle-class French woman. . . . Woman being the weaker creature must harden herself proportionately just that much more to meet the exigencies of her existence.[80]

While Fauset is intent on drawing out generalities about the French in general, she concludes that women suffer even more than men, though she has to resort to gender stereotypes to make her point.

What I find most significant about this essay is that Fauset engages in cultural critique while narrating an experience she is having as a sightseer accompanied by a guide. Although she sets her essay in the context of the marketplace and consumer culture, and begins with details about the profusion of goods and how they are acquired, she writes, "What really held me was the people; all sorts of a given class, with here and there a curious visitor like myself and my friend, but otherwise representatives of the poorer groups of all those nationalities with which Paris teems." She is impressed by the cosmopolitan mix of nationalities, races, and appearances, and is attuned to physical differences, especially the "thin," "swarthy" Kabyles, migrants from North Africa, whose "swarthiness [is] different from that of the Italian, the American mulatto, or the Spaniard," a differentiation of racial characteristics that emphasizes the racial preoccupations of the period. As she leaves the market and its "seething, swarming crowds and the sordid, prosaic wares," Fauset ends with an intriguing mix of images, indicative of her narrative strategy. Behind her lies the market and its myriad goods, but also the fortified ancient city walls "emanat[ing] security, protection," and before her are the "mosque-like towers" of Sacré Coeur, beckoning her to enter as a tourist.[81] True to her pattern, cultural analysis of the meaning of the city wall is couched in the language of poetry and romance and in the context of ordinary travel sights and experiences. Yet her visit to the flea market emphasizes her desire to seek out those sites that are off the beaten path and to make connections with local people and explore local neighborhoods, much as in "Yarrow Revisited." In this way Fauset locates the political and the cultural within, and sets such issues off against, the everyday realities of travel experience.

This pattern is repeated in her March 1925 essay "The Enigma of the Sorbonne," which also begins with a memory. She shares her early recollections of her introduction to the French language in a Sunday newspaper but cannot recall when she first learned that the Sorbonne was the most important university in France. Her inability to distinguish among the chief French universities, a "vagueness [she] find[s] common to most Americans," serves as the impetus for her to write the essay and "penetrate the haze" of American ignorance.[82] While the essay is chiefly a detailed history and description of the Sorbonne, Fauset also alludes to the differences between higher education at the Sorbonne and at an institution such as Tuskegee. A number of articles ran in *The Crisis* emphasizing the higher education that Du Bois privileged in contrast to Washington's vocational educational programs, and the magazine printed pictures of black university graduates and ran many advertisements for colleges, universities, and training schools. Fauset herself graduated from Cornell in 1905 Phi Beta Kappa, the first black student at Cornell and one of the first black women nationwide to be inducted into the honor society.[83]

Her focus on the Sorbonne's educational strengths shifts near the end of the essay to a discussion of its cosmopolitanism. Observing that the Sorbonne does not exhibit the typical "college life" one would expect at an American institution, she describes strolling the grounds, "indulg[ing] [her] great passion," which, she writes, "is to observe and study the appearance, the gestures and such phrases as I can understand of these myriads of students." She watches two Haitian female students who seem unaware of the "extreme tolerance inform[ing] the countenances, yellow, brown, white and ruddy, by which they are surrounded. . . . In this atmosphere so completely are they themselves that tolerance is a quality which they recognize only when they are exercising it toward others."[84] Her comments contrast the acceptance that these women of color enjoy to that which she does not know in the United States but can experience to a greater degree in Europe, where she may take tea in any place she desires. She utilizes the spectacle of these black female bodies and others' reactions to them to make the same point Wells makes about black female mobility and its connection to increased cultural power, but in a more subtle manner and not in reference to her own body. Fauset herself holds the black bodies of the female students in her gaze and uses them in her commentary, thus objectifying them, but she also grants them the sort of subjectivity that she wants to claim for herself. Historical information about the Sorbonne and physical descriptions of the landscape may dominate the essay, but Fauset ultimately wants to penetrate the cultural forces at work beneath the surface details of travel. This foray into cultural work at the end of the essay is characteristic, as I have noted, of her travel pieces.

In the two-part essay "Dark Algiers the White" from the April and May 1925 issues, Fauset presents a more exotic picture of international culture. The first installment begins with her trip to Marseille, where she imagines Algiers and the "dream-land" of Africa beckoning from across a romanticized sea, "lighted at night by stars and constellations which we had never seen; mellowed by a saffron moon climbing from below the surface of the world to the warm, rich velvet of the sky." Upon arriving in Algiers, she employs stereotypical language to describe her immersion in this exotic place: "All the strangeness and difference of that life which, starting far, far in the interior of Africa, yet breaks off so abruptly at the southern edge of the Mediterranean, rose instantly to meet us. Porters agile as monkeys swarmed up narrow rope ladders over the side of the ship," and she disembarks "through a lane of staring chattering faces."[85] As Wall notes, while Fauset's "descriptions of people can be condescending and even racist," she "most often maintains the perspective of respectful outsider" and recognizes that to the residents of Algiers, she is also "exotic."[86] As in her other essays, she invokes her memories as a device to facilitate her travel descriptions and in order to compare her current experience with the more romantic recollections of her earlier travels. In this case she writes that the "white clad patriarchal figures . . . make one think according to his training of pictures seen in Sunday School or film-shown 'Scenes from an Eastern Village,' "[87] suggesting the impact of both religion (a conservative force) and film (a popular culture force) on her travel experiences and further emphasizing the oscillation in Fauset's travel writing between conservative and progressive forces.

This oscillation is also apparent in Fauset's discussion of how East and West meet in Algiers: "Dark figures clad in European clothes but crowned with red fezzes bring East and West together." She includes typical travel details in the essay—a trip on a trolley car, the antics of the conductor, and the colorful sights afforded when she comes upon "mysterious figures of women clothed in white"—but she also inserts critique of gender norms as she watches a woman in a veil with "all but two dark impenetrable eyes and a triangle of creamy forehead" hidden, accompanied by her husband. Of the woman Fauset notes, "Mystery shrouded her; her two eyes stared unseeingly before her; she was like an automaton beside her lord; there was no conversation." When an old woman sits opposite her on the trolley, Fauset examines her veil, which strikes her as "shaped very much like the tiny white apron which a good American housewife sometimes assumes on a leisurely afternoon." Here, however, she resorts to the gender stereotypes with which she is familiar, refusing, perhaps, to take the country on its own terms but insisting that it be filtered through her Western sensibilities; indeed, her suggestion that a veil may operate culturally in the same way one would expect an apron in an American home to mark women's constrained mobility and expression eclipses the larger cultural differences underlying the wearing of the veil. Fauset concludes that the woman's "clothing and her veil lent her mystery and marvel. She was the very savor of the East."[88] In this scene and elsewhere in the essay, Fauset indulges in exoticism and indeed seeks it out in her surroundings, as Stillman did in her identification of the very "soul of Florida."[89] But the next morning in Algiers compromises the romance from the night before: "The merciless sun revealed its defects and destroyed its magic." The clothing is "not quite so white," she writes, and "European trousers and shoes" can be seen below the robes. The children are "sore-eyed," there are many beggars, and "through the voluminous garments of the women showed the outline of misshapen bodies, broken and distorted by neglect, abuse and much bearing of children." Yet, Fauset insists, ultimately "nothing could destroy, could penetrate their air of mystery,"[90] suggesting that she retains a touristic interest in the Algerians' exoticism, much as Stillman holds on to a tourist's perspective until the "shadow" of racial oppression makes it impossible for her to sustain such a point of view.

Fauset further invokes the dichotomy of East and West as she remarks on the difference between the shops on the main thoroughfare, similar to shops on any street in Paris or New York, and those of "the dark and tortuous 'native' quarters," in which "immediately one is in another world." She is relieved to find a more "native" scene off the beaten path, where spectacles of consumer otherness are more appealing to her than the Westernized main streets. She also critiques Westernized images. For example, when "lean and regal" men riding on "Arabian steeds" approach, she laments, "It is too bad that moviedom has spoiled the integrity of this scene; our sophisticated eyes find in it a touch of artificiality."[91] She desires the mundane at the same time that she rejects it for more exotic sights, critiquing the artificially exotic images imposed by film conventions while also seeking and employing such images herself.

Fauset's invocation of U.S. color prejudice follows a similarly ambivalent course. Her introduction to the East Indian owners of "Pohoomull Brothers, Brahmin merchants," allows her to note "a curious phenomenon: the brothers are brown, we are brown, the Arabs are brown, but there is a difference in our brownness, so much so that clad all of us in Western dress, each would shortly be able to discriminate."[92] In reference to the topic of race in Fauset's writings, Wall remarks that this essay, like her fiction, "works to deny the difference that is its most promising subject. . . . [A] too-easy universalism is the clearest evidence of the constraints that constructions of race and gender impose upon Fauset's work."[93] The reference to physical color differences that are apparent only among those in Western dress suggests the nuanced gradations that inform color prejudice in the United States. In this essay and in "This Way to the Flea Market," as discussed earlier, when she indulges in exoticism, Fauset is less aware than we might expect of her own tendencies to stereotype according to what she considers the visible markers of race.

She also exerts cultural superiority as the brothers try to persuade her and her companion to purchase some of the myriad goods in their shop. She repeatedly protests that she has no intention of buying anything, "that we are really quite poor," a problematic position to take as a Westerner in a country that she spends a good deal of time describing as having a standard of living below her own. But the more talkative brother insists "that something in the shape of our heads makes him recognize kindred spirits and that therefore he would do for us what he would do for few others: show us in detail his 3,000,000 francs worth of merchandise and count it time well-spent."[94] This man reminds her of E. M. Forster's Dr. Aziz in *Passage to India* (1924), who believes that "social amenities . . . constitute friendship" and who is overly "eager to please." Fauset's own Orientalism is striking in this passage. The brother tells Fauset and her artist friend that he will try to acquire for them anything they please. When the artist asks for some Moorish women to paint, the man assures him that they frequent his shop, but when the women fail to show up, Fauset says that he, like Forster's Dr. Aziz, "falls down when put to the proof of his protestations."[95]

Fauset concludes the essay in the May 1925 *Crisis,* where she describes herself walking in an area of the city that is potentially unsafe for a woman, a situation that further reveals her cultural ambivalence. She asks a woman in a bakery if it is safe for her to climb farther up the stairs to a higher level of the city. The woman replies, "You may go anywhere, anywhere, Mademoiselle, and then besides one sees that you are from Martinique (Martiniquaise) and there is no danger here for a French woman!" Here, Fauset's presumed racial profile is viewed as something that provides her protection. She continues up the hill and comes upon a small village, "The Court of Miracles," which she describes in terms of the exotic and picturesque: it is filled with "miserable shacks, swarming with women and children. They are unspeakably dirty and ragged yet somehow they strike a picturesque exotic note." Indeed, the scene contains a great deal of color. She writes, "These women are without face veils; one of them passing directly before me wears a head-dress of scarlet, a green jacket with a purple collar, a cerise and yellow skirt," and claims that she "cannot sufficiently describe the picture they made in their gay clothing, the brilliant blue of the sky above, the strong gold of the sun above them, the black background of squalor and wretchedness behind."[96]

Fauset is informed by a woman in the neighborhood that if she "really want[s] to see the natives, how they live," she must go to the Kasbah, the Arab quarter, and here the streets are even more narrow; the houses are so close together that the upper stories touch. Voyeuristically, she looks in open doors, noting the dark and squalid interiors. In this picturesque but dangerous quarter she describes her increasing fear of the Other. As she penetrates into darker and narrower streets, she is "conscious of a slowly mounting fear" and turns toward the sea, where she hopes to find "light and safety."[97] She notes that men look at her as she quickly and resolutely walks out of the district and eventually emerges into bright sunlight.

Her experience in the Kasbah is an interesting blend of her fear of otherness, her sense of vulnerability as a woman caught in the gaze of the men, and her fascination with the dangerous and exotic neighborhood. Her fascination wins out, and she returns the next day with friends, one of whom is Laura Wheeler, who illustrated the article.[98] But because of the warnings of a Frenchwoman who tells her that she should not enter without an escort because of "terrible possible happenings, the tragedies of those sinister, black off-shoots and allies [*sic*],"[99] Fauset decides to return the next day, when the woman's husband, a police officer, can accompany them. Although the husband turns out not to be available the next day, the woman and her daughter take Fauset to several places where they can walk without fear, and in this way, as Wall notes, "the experience of difference, now carefully mediated, is safe."[100]

This is especially true when the woman takes Fauset into Arab homes. Of the first home Fauset remarks, "I am actually in an Arab house in the Kasbah," emphasizing both her opportunity to experience ordinary or "safe" African life and the touristic fascination with and spectacle of "actually" being in an Arab house. Fauset provides a detailed description of this house and others that they visit and their inhabitants, and while her language describes the mundane features of the dwelling, it also implies the spectacle of otherness she finds therein. She notes the listlessness of the women, who sit "doing nothing, absolutely nothing; life slips by." At one point she has a conversation with an older woman with whom she "exchange[s] polite and amiable banalities after the fashion of ladies calling the world over"; indeed, it reminds her of the "politeness . . . of Paris,"[101] and she seems rather surprised that the conventionalities of female social customs are shared by these women. Her description of these homes exemplifies how she experiences both the familiar and the exotic in the Kasbah.

While the Kasbah is frightening in some ways, Fauset's willingness to explore it and her excitement about meeting its residents are significant. Her enthusiasm emphasizes, as Wall observes, that although we might view Fauset as someone who, because of her conservative Methodist childhood, would have been "a reluctant explorer" and whose "spirit of adventure was circumscribed by the demands of propriety," we should also recognize her courageous travel choices, as in her visit to the Kasbah, and the ways that she "encourage[d] exploration and innovation in others."[102] In describing to her readers her willingness to literally step outside her comfort zone, she emphasizes the disordering but exhilarating experiences of mobility. Fauset imposes orderliness on her experience, as Paul Smethurst describes its operation in travel narratives, in her imposition of Western notions of domesticity and gender on the women with whom she has tea. But she also presents a challenge to orderly notions of mobility by emphasizing the threats to her own mobility in the Kasbah.

Smethurst argues that because "travel produces the overlapping of conflicting spaces and temporalities of heterotopias," all travel writing attempts in some way "to bring textual order to bear on the experience of heterotopia produced by travel." This order is "suspended, under erasure" in imperialist travel writing. Fauset manages both to place this tension under erasure and to emphasize its heterotopic power. One of the ways she does this is through her descriptions of her visits to the homes of the Kasbah women. Smethurst claims that "women's travel writing might then be considered disorderly in that it locates women outside their 'proper' place in the domestic sphere of the home culture (doubly at home),"[103] and Fauset emphasizes both the Kasbah women in their homes and herself as transgressing expected boundaries by venturing outside her own domestic space into dangerous territory. Yet the women's homes also function as safe and familiar havens within the dangerous space of the Kasbah; that is, although Fauset is outside her home culture, she does find a domestic space in which to experience this unfamiliar culture. Thus, while her mobility is disorderly, her experience in these homes allows this disorderliness to be contained.

The disorderly nature of mobility resurfaces, however, in Fauset's interactions with her French guide. After her visit to the Kasbah, Fauset does not know how to express her appreciation to the Frenchwoman who has guided her and who refuses any payments or presents. The next day, though, the woman returns to Fauset's door, embarrassed to ask for money to help with the medical expenses of a friend. Fauset is glad to give her some francs, "which she so richly deserves," and notes that "the child says greedily, 'Give them to me maman.'" Finally, "We exchange adieu," Fauset writes, "but our little idyll has a tarnished ending."[104] Even though Fauset tries to compensate the woman immediately after their day together, and seems willing to give her money when she returns the next day—money she "richly deserves"—the implication of begging has "tarnished" her interaction with the woman and her daughter and exposes the disorderly nature of travel in unfamiliar cultural terrain.

Fauset ends the essay the same way she began, invoking a romantic and dreamlike atmosphere and noting that as she sails away, the coast "fades into spray and mist," and "Algiers, Africa, again are dreams."[105] She identifies the essay as having been written from Villefranche-sur-Mer on January 27, 1925, in a manner similar to that of a diary entry, emphasizing the personal and impressionistic nature of the observation. But she also describes and renders exotic the mundane aspects of Algeria—perhaps more overtly here than in any other of her travel essays. As Smethurst observes, exoticism "can never quite be expunged from postcolonial travel narratives when these are aimed principally at western audiences," and this is certainly the case with Fauset's Algerian travel essay. Smethurst argues that travel writers who "have at least one foot outside western culture" use travel writing "as a mode of self-enunciation and cultural exploration. In the process, they are also seeking to extend the discursive boundaries and semantic horizons of the form, and in some cases, to subvert it from within."[106] Fauset is thoroughly engaged in this process, her desire to subvert travel discourse from within established discursive boundaries (such as the domestic) contending with her conservative impulses and her reversion to cultural and racial stereotype.

Fauset's later 1935 *Metropolitan* essay "Episodes in Tangier," capturing some of her experiences from a 1934 trip to Morocco that also included Paris, Gibraltar, Naples, Rome, and Seville, extends these central features of her travel writing and exemplifies her use of these strategies throughout her travel writing career. She begins the essay by noting her desire "to go adventuring into new lands," suggesting her willingness to explore unfamiliar space (such as the Kasbah ten years earlier), but she also complains about seasickness, remarking, "I was not raised to be a sailor." Her discomfort with the unfamiliar space of Gibraltar is mitigated when she bands together with American shipmates to form a shore party; she writes, "Diverse as we all were in interests, age, color and concept we crowded together on the untidy, littered dock, bound by the tie of a common language and a sense that anyone from home was preferable to those strangers with their unknown tongues and different manners."[107]

When they depart the next day for Morocco, she observes that although they have bought second-class tickets, they "ventured over to first class and stayed there without let or hindrance," an interesting allusion to Jim Crow conditions in the United States, where not only was such blurring of social boundaries illegal but also even spaces supposedly guaranteed to black travelers might be restricted by the caprice of a porter or ticket seller. Once in Tangier, she notices the "general picturesqueness of the porters" and notes that "the British calm," "efficiency," and "orderliness" of Gibraltar have disappeared. In contrast to Algiers, "where one is constantly reminded of France," here there is "so much to see, so much color, so much life, so much decidedly un-European"; clearly a disorderly mobility has replaced the order of Algiers or Gibraltar. Fauset and her travel companions are drawn to cultural spectacle, and when coming upon a speaker addressing a crowd, they press closer, "hoping and fearing that they might be assisting at some ritual, some exorcism of evil spirits, some quaint and different manifestation of Oriental belief and practice." When a young clergyman in their party attempts to take a photograph, the speaker and the crowd angrily approach Fauset's group. The incident does not result in confrontation, but later, over "a reassuring game of bridge," Fauset muses, "None of us knew how near we might have been to disaster that afternoon."[108]

She concludes the essay by describing her chance meeting with two friends who now live in Morocco and entertain her for the afternoon. The disturbing scene in the public square is all but forgotten as she walks in her friends' garden, the steps of which "led in a gentle slope from the pinky-white marble of the house through tender trees to the sparkling blue of the strait of Gibraltar." The familiarity of Gibraltar and old friends restores order to her experience and to the essay. Indeed, the adventure, danger, and exotic nature of her time in Tangier are eclipsed in the last section of the essay as she enjoys the middle-class calm of bridge and a garden walk. Yet it is also important to acknowledge Fauset's willingness to explore her discomfort and her unease. While she restores a sense of safe familiarity at the essay's end, she has also allowed readers to witness her unease. And as she represents her and her companions' cultural ignorance during the incident in the public square, she admits her embarrassment: when the crowd turns away, she describes her party as "considerably abashed" and attempting to leave the scene "with what dignity we could muster."[109] These small gestures of cultural humility also represent part of the important cultural work that Fauset undertakes in her travel essays. While her mobility allows her to impose a measure of order upon these exotic scenes, she sometimes expresses a traveling identity that overcomes these attitudes to demonstrate the truly liberating aspects of travel and to embrace its inherently disorderly mobility.

5

BODIES OF KNOWLEDGE

Cultural Authority and Black Female Mobility in Zora Neale Hurston's *Tell My Horse*

Discussing the role of the body in travel texts, Marguerite Helmers and Tilar J. Mazzeo note that travel writers have employed the "implied presence of the body" as a way to guarantee that their travel accounts are authentic and are based on " 'first-hand' or 'eye-witness' experience."[1] As I noted in chapter 1, theories of the gaze suggest that scopic desire leads to the erasure of the seeing body to focus on the gaze itself, which, often emanating from the white male body of the colonizer, becomes an ideological apparatus of empire in travel texts, as Mary Louise Pratt discusses in *Imperial Eyes* (2008). As Lila Harper and Sara Mills remind us, issues of corporeality become quite complex for women writers or writers of color, whose actual bodies can be read as visible signs of difference,[2] as demonstrated by Ida B. Wells's deployment of her visible and mobile black body to accomplish her antilynching agenda. In *Tell My Horse* (1938), Zora Neale Hurston also emphasizes her visibility as a woman of color and her mobility as a traveler, but she does so in order to record and transmit cultural knowledge about the Caribbean. In March 1936 Hurston was awarded a Guggenheim fellowship to study religious practices in the West Indies. She arrived in Jamaica in April and then traveled to Haiti, where she wrote *Their Eyes Were Watching God* in seven weeks.[3] She returned to the United States in March 1937 and then traveled back to Haiti in May after her fellowship was renewed. She concluded her research and returned to the United States in the fall of the same year, and *Tell My Horse* was published in October 1938. Through her travel experiences and text, Hurston resists the erasure of her body as she links her status as a black female traveler to the transmission of stories, histories, and cultural practices in the Caribbean, emphasizing in the process the integral relationship of folklore to individual and cultural identity in the African diaspora.

As she gains cultural competency during her time in Jamaica and Haiti, she also acquires authority to act as an agent of preservation. At one point in *Tell My Horse,* she notes that while she does not know the "people and Creole" as well as she would like to, she does know ethnographic "methods." The more time she spends in the Caribbean, however, the more knowledge she acquires. She learns Creole and becomes a cultural insider as she hears of Haitian "secret societies," is mentored by houngans and mambos (male and female voodoo priests),[4] and gains the confidence of other community leaders. In her letters from the field, Hurston discusses her acquisition of insider status; indeed, she claims that she has "no trouble at all in making [herself] understood," that she is witness to cultural events that have been experienced by very few people outside of the community, and that the people are beginning to like her and "seek [her] out to tell [her] things."[5] Hurston's ability to achieve such insider status exists in interesting tension with her detractors' remarks that she is ill-equipped for such research.

Ultimately, the movement of Hurston's physical body functions as a trope for the ways in which bodies of cultural knowledge might travel or be transmitted and preserved. Significantly, Hurston's acts of travel and writing contradict the limited mobility and diminished subjectivity generally associated with the history of black women's travel, particularly during slavery. In relation to the Middle Passage, Hurston's experiences cause us to rethink assumptions about the black bodies and identities of slaves in transit, which are sometimes viewed as "literally suspended" in the "*nowhere*" and the "undiffentiated identity" of the Atlantic, to use Hortense J. Spillers's terms. In her discussion of the "dehumanizing, ungendering, and defacing" aspects of the Middle Passage, Spillers stresses the ways in which the slave trade profoundly reworked the meanings of mobility and identity, as well as how difficult it has become to think beyond these paradigms.

Hurston's travel experiences challenge conventional thinking about black female mobility by emphasizing the power of black women to transmit both their physical bodies and cultural bodies of knowledge across the space of the Atlantic. Hurston's specific focus on the agency of a mobile black female body is even more significant in light of the notion, according to Spillers's paradigm, that differentiation between male and female bodies breaks down in the Middle Passage. Spiller contends that while the female slave may occupy less physical space in the "directly translatable money economy" of a slave ship, she becomes ungendered in part because she is still "quantifiable by the same rules of accounting as her male counterpart."[6] Hurston's narrative, however, highlights the specifically gendered experience of black mobility.[7] Indeed, through the liberated mobility and cultural work of her Caribbean travels, and in opposition to the dehumanizing paradigms of both the slave journey and Jim Crow racism, Hurston's narrative allows us to reimagine the Atlantic world as a space that mobilizes and authorizes black female bodies to participate in the collection and transmission of cultural knowledge.

Hurston emphasizes the authority of her fieldwork and its textual artifacts through her eyewitness account of and physical participation in Jamaican and Haitian culture. In a departure from the objective observer method of her mentor Franz Boas, Hurston chose to work as a participant observer. While this does not necessarily represent a new ethnographic persona, *Tell My Horse* explores the important question of what it means when a black woman occupies this position. Critical estimations of Hurston's approach reveal some uncertainty about how to address this question; indeed, scholarship on her ethnography exhibits confusion about how best to characterize her work and, most significantly, a reluctance to grant her professional authority. For example, scholars have described Hurston's methods as "improvising ethnography," "biculturalism," or, in even more negative terms, "exuberant" but a function of her "erratic temperament" and ultimately unprofessional.[8] This last description is similar to the reasons given by Edwin Embree, president of the Julius Rosenwald Fund, for reducing Hurston's fellowship to pay for her education at Columbia. In what amounted to a personality clash, Embree complained to Boas about the general "tumult" of Hurston's life, her self-promotion, and her inability to pursue "serious quiet scholarship."[9] Apparently there was little room within the dominant institutional and cultural frameworks of the early twentieth century for Hurston's bold and unconventional voice. Indeed, given some of the more recent estimations of her work, it is apparent that her voice continues to be viewed as disruptive. Such characterizations negatively affected Hurston's scholarly pursuits and her critical reception.

These sorts of critical reactions are also reflected in the reception of *Their Eyes Were Watching God* (1937), which Hurston composed during her Caribbean travels. The novel was viewed with varying degrees of negativity by African American reviewers, who were concerned about its supposed lack of depth and its primitive or exotic portrait of African American culture, particularly in light of how white audiences might read it. In his October 1937 *New Masses* review of the novel, Richard Wright famously dismisses Hurston's prose as being "cloaked in that facile sensuality that has dogged Negro expression since the days of Phillis Wheatley." Wright concludes that Hurston has pandered to the "chauvinistic tastes" of her white audience by perpetuating "the tradition which was *forced* upon the Negro in the theater, that is, the minstrel technique that makes the 'white folks' laugh."[10] Similarly, Ralph Ellison declares that Hurston's novel "retains the blight of calculated burlesque that has marred most of her writing."[11] And while Otis Ferguson notes in his *New Republic* review that the novel is "absolutely free of Uncle Toms," he also suggests that "a tangle of lush exposition and overblown symbols" drowns out its action and feeling; despite his recognition of the novel's "gold mine of traditional sayings," he concludes that the dialect is "sloppy."[12] Alain Locke in *Opportunity* labels the novel "folklore fiction" and claims that Hurston oversimplifies her characters and their cultural milieu.[13] Hurston responds to Locke's charge that the novel does not represent serious social document fiction by countering in her 1938 essay "Art and Such," written for the Florida Federal Writers' Project, that she knows from her personal experience and depicts in her fictional work that black people "love and hate and fight and play and strive and travel and have a thousand and one interests in life like other humans." Furthermore, she criticizes the self-appointed "Race Leader[s]" who, when noting white people's "curiosity about some activity among Negroes . . . offered themselves as an authority on the subject whether they have ever heard of it before or not."[14] Such statements relate directly to the argument that she makes in *Tell My Horse* about the importance of her own firsthand experience and cultural authority while challenging the so-called expertise of her critics.

The white mainstream press was more positive in its judgment of *Their*

Eyes, but some of these positive appraisals emphasize the novel's exoticism, which was exactly the reaction that several of Hurston's black critics feared. For example, George Stevens notes the "rich, racy, and authentic" lives of Hurston's characters in Eatonville, Florida, and again, later in the review, writes that "no one has ever reported the speech of Negroes with a more accurate ear for its raciness, its rich invention, and its music."[15] Lucy Tompkins claims in the *New York Times Book Review* that the novel is about "every [Negro] . . . who isn't so civilized that he has lost the capacity for glory,"[16] and Sheila Hibben declares that the novel contains a "gleaming riot of black people, with a limitless exuberance of humor, and a wild, strange sadness," even as she praises Hurston's ability to write "with her head as well as with her heart" and avoid being "too much preoccupied with the current fetish of the primitive."[17] The underlying condescension in such reviews suggests that even positive criticism of Hurston's work attempted to regulate the substance and timbre of her voice.

Hurston's own statements about her work in the Caribbean indicate the power of cultural narratives and influential individuals that suggest she should restrain her voice. From Port-au-Prince, Haiti, on January 6, 1937, in her postscript to an already lengthy letter to Henry Allen Moe (who was overseeing her Guggenheim fellowship), Hurston admits that she has not included all her activities in her report, explaining, "I tried that in the first version of the letter and it only succeeded in looking like I was too *mouthy.*" Just as she sometimes downplays her expertise in *Tell My Horse,* the self-deprecation in the letter is subtle but important for the way in which it indicates her internalization of negative cultural messages about black women's voices and authority. Yet her letters also contain passages that demonstrate her resistance to the restraints placed on her voice and work. For example, writing to Melville Herskovits on April 6, 1937, from New York, she undermines the authority of those who would silence her, such as Embree, by expressing her lack of "faith in [Embree's] equipment as an anthropologist." And in an earlier letter to Herskovits on July 30, 1936, from Accompong Town, Jamaica, Hurston enumerates the ways in which the work she has instigated on her own answers important questions about Jamaican culture, perhaps as a challenge to his advice that, given her inadequate grasp of Creole, she leave Jamaica and concentrate on the Bahamas instead. In a September 24, 1936, letter to Moe, Hurston also complains that Charles S. Johnson and Herskovits were advancing the career of Katherine

Dunham (a U.S. dancer, choreographer, and anthropologist of dance who studied with Herskovits and whom Hurston regarded as a rival) by "suppressing" Hurston, and in letters to Moe and Herskovits, Hurston highlighted Dunham's limitations as an anthropologist in contrast to her own attention to detail. In these letters Moe comes across as sympathetic to the power and authority of Hurston's voice, insisting, in response to Hurston's tendency to address him as "bossman," that the fellowship holders were the "bosses" of their own work. Apparently Moe had asked about the female equivalent for "busha" (Jamaican for "boss"), to which Hurston replied that there was no such word, given women's lack of position in Jamaica, but she thanked him for his compliment in viewing her in such a light.[18]

Hurston more explicitly emphasized her disciplinary expertise in a letter to Herskovits written April 15, 1936, from Kingston, Jamaica, in which she noted the lack of "real curricula" for anthropologists who wanted to study African American culture and her belief that she "could bring more to the Dept." at Columbia than "it could give [her] in the matter."[19] Such passages in her letters reveal Hurston's growing awareness of her own authority as a researcher during her time in the Caribbean, and similarly positive evaluations of Hurston's voice and methods appear in the work of recent scholars. Deborah Plant notes Hurston's innovative fieldwork in Florida, Louisiana, Alabama, and the Caribbean; Kevin Meehan emphasizes "the important contributions Hurston makes to the theory and practice of anthropological writing and cultural decolonization" in *Tell My Horse;* Tiffany Ruby Patterson characterizes Hurston as an "expert witness to the 'genius of the common people' " and to "the imaginative worlds of black people in the twentieth century"; and Alice Walker famously refers to Hurston as a "native American genius."[20] Despite these affirmative appraisals of Hurston's important contributions to our understanding of African American and African Caribbean culture, none of Hurston's critics have considered her unique approach and style, both in the field and within the genre of the travel text, as a function of her physical mobility.[21] Approaching Hurston's text as a travel narrative challenges criticism of its form, such as in Robert E. Hemenway's assertion that *Tell My Horse* is Hurston's "poorest book" because she was not a seasoned "traveloguist,"[22] and emphasizes Hurston's mobility as a key component of the cultural authority that she assumes while in the Caribbean.

Early in the Jamaican sections of the text, Hurston links issues of authority to her national, racial, gender, and professional identities as they coincide with her physically mobile self. She initiates this discussion by delineating the influence of colonial culture in Jamaica's hierarchies of color and caste. She notes that in most cases, the parents of mixed-race individuals have not been "properly married" and "the mixed-blood bears the name with the bar sinister." But such an individual also "has prestige, no matter how he happened to come by his light skin." Hurston muses that "perhaps the Jamaican mixed bloods are logical and right, perhaps the only answer to the question of what is to become of the negro in the Western world is that he must be absorbed by the whites." If this is the case, she continues, then the approach taken by blacks in the United States—that is, working to achieve equality in relation to whites but retain a separate racial identity—may be "all wrong." If this absorption into the white race is what must be done, "then any way at all of getting more whiteness among us is a step in the right direction." She may mean the comment facetiously, and she sidesteps responsibility for it by claiming that she does not "pretend to know what is wise and best,"[23] but in any case, it is a curious statement and has the potential, given its ambivalence, to anger both her allies and her enemies.

We could read the statement alongside the conclusion of *Dust Tracks on a Road* (1942), where she similarly engages issues of color in a way that could suggest both acquiescence in and resistance to white superiority:

> So I give you [whites] all my right hand of fellowship and love, and hope for the same for you. In my eyesight, you lose nothing by not looking just like me. I will remember you all in my good thoughts, and I ask you kindly to do the same for me. . . . You, who play the zig-zag lightning of power over the world, . . . think kindly of those who walk in the dust. And you who walk in humble places, think kindly too, of others. There has been no proof in the world so far that you would be less arrogant, if you held the lever of power in your hands.[24]

Hemenway observes how Hurston shifts the perspective in this concluding passage of her autobiography to suggest that whites "do not have to feel inferior just because they do not look like her," thus exposing "the absurdity of the white norm."[25] Although Hurston's comments in *Tell My Horse* about "getting more whiteness among us" could be read as an acceptance of color prejudice, it also exposes the illogical nature of race prejudice and critiques the fixation on color in both the white and black communities.

Hurston's statement about the infusion of whiteness into the black race also underscores her own experience as a mixed-race woman confronting

Jamaica's complicated attitudes toward issues of color. Hurston's father, John Hurston, was a mulatto preacher and mayor of Eatonville, and Hurston would explore the complex experience of mixed-race individuals in Florida in *Their Eyes.* In the novel, Hurston's character Janie relates the story of her enslaved grandmother's rape by the white master and her beating by the white mistress when her light-skinned and gray-eyed child is born. Another representation of mixed-race issues appears in the character of Mrs. Turner, the light-skinned woman who despises Janie's blackness, berates her for marrying the dark-skinned Tea Cake, and argues that mixed-race individuals such as herself and Janie should "lighten up" the race by marrying white people.[26] In *Tell My Horse,* Hurston invokes this range of attitudes toward mixed-race experience when she discusses color prejudice in Jamaica. She writes that the desire of Jamaicans to become more white is "a curious spectacle to the eyes of an American Negro," and she feels as if she has "stepped back to the days of slavery or the generation immediately after surrender" in the United States.[27]

Indeed, the racial atmosphere in Jamaica contains both promise and threat and suggests some of the physical realities of racism in the United States during and after Reconstruction, such as segregation, passing, and lynching, aspects of race relations to which Hurston alludes through her references to the mixing of white and black blood. Ida B. Wells provides powerful illustrations of some of these realities in her late nineteenth-century antilynching and travel texts, as I discussed in chapter 1. Wells notes in her antilynching discourse that the alleged rape of white women by black men is used as justification for lynching,[28] when in reality such rape charges were motivated by a more complex set of issues. As Robyn Wiegman aptly states, "the loss of miscegenation's economic rationalization under slavery turns the question of interracial sexuality toward the more tension-wrought domain of sexual desire," and the "myth of the black male rapist serves to compensate for this economic loss."[29] Mason Stokes notes that by attacking the connections between interracial rape and lynching, Wells also returned to white women "an agency denied them in . . . the 'rape mythos.' "[30] Of course, as Hurston's *Their Eyes* and many other fictional and nonfictional accounts reveal, on the other side of this issue lies the horrific repeated rape of black women slaves by white masters. Hurston raises the issue of miscegenation and all that it represents about the oppression of African Americans in general and African American women in particular both during and after slavery when she draws attention to the color prejudice in Jamaica. She offers a particularly compelling example of such prejudice, and one that clearly invokes histories and discourses of U.S. slavery, in her criticism of the Jamaican practice of rendering black mothers of mixed-race persons invisible (these women are not "mentioned or exhibited") so that an individual's white paternity can be emphasized, no matter how "questionable the circumstances of birth."[31] Indeed, in addition to the discourses of rape, lynching, and segregation that this example alludes to, it reminds readers of the stipulation that the children of slave women follow the status of the mother, ensuring the "displacement of the black female's maternity within the slave system" and "guaranteeing paternal rights and privileges as definitively white racial ones."[32]

Because Hurston's accounts of intra-racial color prejudice and black female oppression reveal the exclusion of and violence against the black female population in Jamaica while invoking past and present racial realities in the United States, such references emphasize the important cultural associations that Hurston forges in her travel narrative and which she links to the movement of her own black body and her project of Caribbean cultural transmission and preservation. For example, she observes that Jamaican blacks are beginning to have more respect for their cultural heritage, and she registers this respect through their love of "their own things," namely, songs, stories, proverbs, and dances.[33] Through her role as recorder and preserver of such "things" as she travels throughout the country, her familiarity with a similar period of transition in the relationship between oppressor and oppressed in the United States, and her own racial experiences and identity, Hurston establishes her authority as a black female traveler and ethnographer who contributes to the counter-narrative against black oppression and disenfranchisement in Jamaica.[34]

In support of this counter-narrative, she highlights the degree to which she transgresses the logic of gender in her travel and work. Frances Bartkowski, building on Mary Louise Pratt's contention that women travelers are "not to be seen seeing," argues that Hurston in fact represents herself as such.[35] A compelling example of this strategy occurs when Hurston offers an interpretation of what she has seen and experienced as an American woman in Haiti:

> It is a curious thing to be a woman in the Caribbean after you have been a woman in these United States. . . . The majority of men in all the states are pretty much agreed that just for being born a girl-baby you ought to have laws and privileges and pay and perquisites. And so far as being allowed to voice opinions is concerned, why, they consider that you are born with the

> law in your mouth, and that is not a bad arrangement either. . . .
>
> But now Miss America, World's champion woman, you take your promenading self down into the cobalt blue waters of the Caribbean and see what happens. You meet a lot of darkish men who make vociferous love to you, but otherwise pay you no mind. If you try to talk sense, they look at you pitifully as if to say, "What a pity! That mouth that was made to supply some man . . . with kisses, is spoiling itself asking stupidities about banana production and wages!" It is not that they try to put you in your place, no. They consider that you never had any.[36]

Hurston's analysis not only draws attention to her gaze as a female traveler but also implies that she understands the gendered consequences and contexts of what she has seen and grasps the differences existing between her and Caribbean women.

Kevin Meehan argues that Hurston's statement "after you have been a woman in these United States" captures both the privilege (in comparison with the status of her native female informants in the Caribbean) and oppression of women in the United States. Hurston's silence about this oppression serves as a "gendered silent crux" in the text, recognized by those who understand the predicament of U.S. women, and thus an example of Hurston's "self-ironizing rhetoric" throughout the text. Meehan notes that such rhetoric "validate[s] [Hurston's] descriptions of women's experiences in the Caribbean by making clear Hurston's awareness that she occupies a different location within the social machinery of imperialism" from that of her female informants. In contrast, Eve E. Dunbar argues that treating Hurston's racial and gender politics as ironic "invites a too-positive critical intervention" and instead claims that Hurston is "unwilling to permit that modern womanhood is possible outside the confines of the United States." Because Hurston is "bound by" and "invested in" U.S. "notions of modernity and power" that support her commitment to the "project of black belonging and citizenship within the United States," Dunbar concludes that her representation of Caribbean gender politics is undertaken in service of this project and at the expense of Caribbean women.[37]

Hurston further complicates her gender critique by staging a dialectic of her own womanliness and professionalism, a feature also found in Wells's and Fauset's travel writing, and illustrated when she experiences the misogynistic attitude described in the passage just quoted while attending a curry goat feed in her honor in St. Mary's parish. She notes that the event is "utterly masculine in every detail" and something "that [had] never been done for another woman." The goat feed also includes a storytelling contest, with songs and "humorous pokes and jibes at each other," reminiscent of the mule stories in which Janie attempts to participate in *Their Eyes.* A few days later, voicing sentiments similar to those of Jody Starks in *Their Eyes,* a young man from St. Mary's tells Hurston that he believes that "women who went in for careers were just so mu[ch] wasted material. American women, he contended, were destroyed by their brains." He feels it is "a great tragedy to look at American women[,] whom he thought the most beautiful and vivacious on earth, and then to think what little use they were as women." Hurston hurls rejoinders about women's achievements and men's limitations to counter the patriarchal ideology underpinning his arguments, but she finds that she must adopt a passive attitude of listening rather than talking in order to gain his trust so that he will share his cultural knowledge with her.[38] Thus, while Hurston enjoys a degree of freedom in her gender and physical mobility that allows her to attend a goat feed in her honor, she also feels the need to feign a passive role in her conversation with the young man in order to achieve her purposes.

In another example of this dialectic, as the only woman in a hog hunting party, she remarks that she carried her "camera and note book," emphasizing her professional identity. But she also feels compelled to tell her readers that she brought along "a few little womanish things like comb and tooth brush and a towel," a nod to gender norms. Her ironic stance toward such norms is most apparent when she observes what a "curious thing" it is to be a woman in the Caribbean after having experienced great privilege as a woman in the United States.[39] The statement is ironic given her exploration in her other writing of black women's distinct lack of privilege in the United States. In *Their Eyes,* for example, Hurston examines two extremes of women's oppression: Logan Killicks wants to hitch Janie to a mule while Jody Starks wants her sitting silent and immobile on the front porch of his store. Even though her relationship with Tea Cake is much more positive, Janie can only fully embrace her subjectivity after she shoots the rabid Tea Cake and endures a murder trial. In her first published story, "The Gilded Six-Bits," Hurston also explores the unconventional steps women must take in order to exert power and take control of their lives; in the story she critiques women's lack of access to economic power through Missie May's commodification of her body so she may acquire the gold coins that her husband, Joe, desires.[40] Hurston herself serves as an example of the necessity for women to be active participants in their own lives when she relates in *Dust Tracks on a Road* how difficult it was for her to deal with her lover's attitude that he should do all the giving in the relationship and she should be content to remain "on the receiving end."[41] The tension between women's agency and dependence is thus apparent throughout Hurston's life experiences and writing.

In the Caribbean, Hurston observes, women's inferior status is further compounded by the fact that class and color prejudice absolve men of all cultural obligations to women outside of their class. Considering women's work, she notes that a Caribbean woman "can do the same labors as a man or a mule and nobody thinks anything about it. . . . [These women] look so wretched with their bare black feet all gnarled and distorted from walking barefooted over rocks. The nails on their big toes thickened like a hoof." As an ethnographer, she might participate in the objective collecting of these disturbing data about the plight of Caribbean women, but sometimes she does so with a strategically ironic or detached air that perhaps suggests her disagreement with cultural norms, as in her noticeably disconnected account of the older Jamaican women, "specialists" of love, who prepare younger women's bodies and minds for the sexual duties of marriage.[42] Given that she was trained by Boas in the "indiscriminate and extensive" collection of cultural lore,[43] we might read her detachment here as an attempt to achieve the objectivity ensured by the Boasian field methodology.

Her omission of details about these women is telling, however, and may also reveal, as Shealeen Meaney contends, the fact that Hurston does not "embed herself in women's communities" but instead seeks opportunities "to circulate in otherwise male-only realms" and perhaps gain insider knowledge that women do not have access to. At the same time, Hurston is able as a black American woman "to access realms of domesticity and personal life that might be closed off to male anthropologists,"[44] and she does refer to some of the women she meets as friends. Though she spends considerable time with the female "love specialists," she does not record their names or describe in much detail her interactions with them, as she sometimes does when she recounts other cultural practices, including those related to voodoo.[45] This ambivalence implies her obligations and loyalties as a black female traveler, ethnographer, and writer, and we could read her narrative stance as an indication to her reader of her disapproval of such cultural norms given her strong comments elsewhere in the text about women's oppression in the region.

In addition to her selective portrayal of cultural practices, Hurston is also strategic in her disclosure of information about herself, both to her readers and to those with whom she associates in the Caribbean. Sometimes she withholds information about her own expertise and refuses to disclose her methods to those around her while at other times she is candid with the reader about the limitations of her research. Controlling this information represents one of the ways in which black women ethnographers and travelers are able to establish self and cultural authority and exercise power. In doing so, Hurston emphasizes how important it is for women to assume responsibility for their own empowerment while underscoring the difficulties of such a project.

For example, she seeks to emphasize women's sexual power in Haitian culture but must avoid objectifying women in the process, a conundrum that coincides with her own experience as a black female ethnographer and is reminiscent of her approach to the Jamaican "love specialists." Explaining the approach to female sexual power in the culture, she writes that Erzulie Freida, mulatto goddess of love, is "the ideal of the love bed. . . . The Virgin Mary and all the female saints of the Church have been elevated, and celebrated for their abstinence. [But] Erzulie is worshipped for her perfection in giving herself to mortal man." In the process of commending Erzulie to her readers, Hurston refers both to her own authority as eyewitness researcher and to the limits of her study. She notes, "Nobody in Haiti ever really told me who Erzulie Freida was, but they told me what she was like and what she did." She describes in detail the ceremony for initiation into the cult of Erzulie though it is never clear if she herself witnessed such a ceremony. She does, however, emphasize her eyewitness gaze while relating the scene of a ceremony and objects related to it: "I have stood in one of the bedrooms, decorated and furnished for a visit from the [goddess]." She also writes of her limitations, noting her imaginative effort to visualize the effects of the ceremony as she "look[s] at the little government employee standing [in the bedroom] amid the cut flowers, the cakes, the perfumes and the lace covered bed." Thanks to "the spur of imagination," Hurston writes, she "saw his common clay glow with some borrowed light and his earthiness transfigured as he mated with a goddess that night." Perhaps in defense of her lack of access to an actual ceremony, she acknowledges that her narrative "does not pretend to give a full account of either voodoo or voodoo gods," which would require volumes. She is "merely attempting to give an effect of the whole in the round."[46]

Hurston's descriptions of these various cultural practices were viewed by some contemporary reviewers as sensational. Harold Courlander in the *Saturday Review* noted that the book "is a curious mixture of remembrances, travelogue, sensationalism, and anthropology. The remembrances are vivid, the travelogue tedious, the sensationalism reminiscent of [William] Seabrook, and the anthropology a melange of misinterpretation and exceedingly good folk-lore. . . . There is a constant conflict between anthropological truth and tale-telling . . . [and] there is a general feeling that the material was not completely digested."[47] A *New Republic* reviewer resorted to stereotype to refer to the text as "mumbojumbo translated for Americans, but still accompanied by the beat of the tom-toms."[48] Alain Locke characterized parts of the text as "anthropological gossip" and declared that the book did not qualify as "social documentation" or even "scientific folk-lore" because it is "too shot through with personal reactions and the piquant thrills of a travelogue."[49] Genevieve M. West notes that when the book failed to appeal to readers desiring a more scientific approach, the publisher advertised it as a memoir or travel narrative, and some of this advertising emphasized the book's sensationalism.[50]

By contrast, an October 12, 1938, review in the *New York Times Book Review* and a December 7, 1938, review in *New Republic* both remarked on the text's absence of sensationalism, and Carter G. Woodson admires Hurston's unique and important work in his review in the *Journal of Negro History*, where he claims that "Hurston is 'almost *sui generis.*' "[51] Hurston's successes and challenges as a professional and as a woman, and as both empowered and feminine, are all in play in such passages, as they are for the figure of Erzulie or any woman who negotiates the thorny issues of gender and authority. Indeed, rather than viewing Hurston's descriptions of Caribbean culture as sensational, we should consider how they allow her to emphasize the gendered experience of her travels and the level of self-authorization in which she participates, bringing, as Frances Bartkowski notes, "her own mystification to light" and representing herself as "seen seeing."[52]

The complex work of the black female ethnographer, as well as the power of Hurston's position, is further illustrated by one of her photos featuring several women, "The Mambo Offers to Damballa" (fig. 2), which is an interesting study in the web of gazes that Hurston herself negotiates. As

Bartkowski argues, some of the rhetorical power of Hurston's text derives from the fact that "readers have indeed seen . . . [her] seeing, and have come to know [her] knowing."[53] The level of visual and intellectual authority that Hurston establishes for herself in the text is succinctly symbolized in the photo. First, we notice the gaze of the camera, emanating from Hurston herself as photographer and observer. Her readers who view the photo also stand in this subject position. Initially, the viewer's eyes are likely drawn to a woman in a white dress holding a white chicken who figures prominently from the middle to the right-hand side of the photo. This woman looks to the left, and so the viewer's gaze follows her gaze to a woman with a basket on her head. Finally, viewers notice a young woman in the lower right of the photo looking up at the photographer-observer, placing viewers in the object position of her gaze. Even though there are photos of men in the book, this image emphasizes women as objects of the viewer's (and of one another's) gaze but also as transmitters of the gaze, positions that Hurston herself negotiates as a black female ethnographer, traveler, and travel writer.

I noted at the beginning of the chapter that the elision of the role of the physical body in the processes of traveling and seeing grants ideological power to what Mary Louise Pratt terms the imperial gaze emanating from the white male colonizing body. As Marguerite Helmers and Tilar Mazzeo argue, the "implied presence" of the traveler's body grants a degree of power to the travel text as an authentic firsthand account though, as Pratt shows in *Imperial Eyes,* the traveling imperial body is usually gendered as male.[54] Hurston disrupts both of these dominant paradigms through her emphasis in the narrative on her own mobile black female body and her authoritative gaze. Indeed, whereas, according to Radhika Mohanram, the erasure of the body in anthropological and historical discourse often acts as a sign of imperial power and access to knowledge of the object,[55] Hurston emphasizes the presence of her black female body and her gaze as signs of cultural power and access to cultural knowledge.

There are important moments in the text when Hurston clearly asserts the kind of authority reserved for a gazing subject. Sometimes she does so through the control of information about herself. When she visits the Maroons at Accompong, ruled by a Colonel Rowe, she senses that he has questions about her motives, but she does not tell him what they are. He offers to stage a dance for her, but she declines, again not telling him that she was "too old a hand at collecting to fall for staged-dance affairs," in

FIGURE 2. "The Mambo Offers to Damballa." Source: Zora Neale Hurston, *Tell My Horse* (1938).

both cases emphasizing her professional expertise and her advantage in the situation. If she cannot witness a cultural practice "in its natural setting and sequence," she says, "I do not bother." In an interesting counterpoint to her mobility, she knows that if she asks for something specifically, she will get it out of context, so she sometimes "sat around and waited" for authentic experience and information to come her way.[56] Soon after she arrives in Haiti in 1936, she notes in an undated letter to Henry Moe that her approach is to "just squat down awhile and after that things begin to happen."[57] Dunbar views Hurston's willingness to wait for authentic or "primitive" experiences as an indication of her passivity and Western biases,[58] but I read this approach as further support for her authority as a traveler. Ethnography, as Hurston represents it, seems to require both mobility and stasis, and in either case, Hurston frequently withholds information about herself or her methods, thus emphasizing her control over her identity and a level of agency not generally afforded to black women during the period.

At other times, Hurston asserts her subjectivity through the degree to which she physically participates in Haitian cultural practice, particularly in regard to voodoo. Her role as a participant observer, even as an initiate observer as she goes through a Canzo ceremony (the penultimate step toward the voodoo priesthood), provides her with an impressive degree of access to the religion and its adherents. Furthermore, her Creole improves and she interacts in an easy and familiar way with other participants in the ceremonies. While participating in these ceremonies, Hurston makes an important distinction between the scholarly opinion of the educational establishment and her own field experience. She writes that the people she observes sing "Papa Legba" in their songs, but the scholars point out that the African word is actually "Lecbah" or "Letbah." "Perhaps the people are in error," she says; "*All I know* is that they sing 'Papa Legba.' "[59] In this way she privileges her own firsthand observation, her own body, eyes, and ears registering the realities of the ceremony and its actual practice rather than the scholarly explanation of it. Yet she is careful to make clear that despite her immersion in Caribbean cultural practice, she has not been converted to voodoo in a way that would compromise her objectivity. In her January 6, 1937, letter to Moe summarizing her experience in Haiti thus far, she observes that Haitian religion has "captured many white people who have not gotten so far," she says, "as I have in the mysteries." Fearing that he might misunderstand her having a set of ceremonial drums baptized and named for him, she assures him, "No I have not been converted locally, tho I am not a christian either."[60] She wants Moe to understand that she is able to be both immersed in and yet objective about the culture.

Her emphasis on the extensive field knowledge that she acquires through this approach challenges the supposedly greater authority of professional ethnographers against whom one of her early biographers, Robert Hemenway, defined Hurston's looser ethnographic practice.[61] As another example of the detailed cultural knowledge that she acquires, she includes long lists of gods and chants that she herself recites in ceremonies. Her use of so much space in her narrative for this excess detail (to which, as she argues in her letter to Moe, she is unable to do justice in a letter, as "it is like explaining the planetary theory on a postage stamp") emphasizes two aspects of her approach: first, collecting and recording such evidence as part of established ethnographic "methods" aligns her work with that of other professionals such as her teacher-mentor Franz Boas; and second, the eyewitness nature of this detail grants her authority because of her physical participation in the religion.[62]

Her experience with Zombies in Haiti further illustrates the function of authority in her text. She begins her chapter on the subject by raising the question of the veracity of Zombies and, in the process, about the nature of her work (and indeed all ethnographic work) in general. She is inherently interested in how the ethnographer arrives at the truth. "What is the whole truth . . . about Zombies?" she asks. "I do not know, but I know that I *saw* the broken remnant, relic, or refuse of Felicia Felix-Mentor in a hospital yard."[63] In her autobiography she writes that her "greatest thrill was coming face to face with a Zombie and photographing her . . . [something that] had never happened before in the history of man."[64] Hurston includes this photo in *Tell My Horse* (fig. 3), and through the photo and her emphasis on the singular occasion of photographing such an individual, she emphasizes the unique and important qualities of her project. Although the Haitian upper classes call Zombies a myth, she claims: "I had the rare opportunity to see and touch an authentic case. I listened to the broken noises in its throat, and then, I did what no one else had ever done, I photographed it. If I had not experienced all of this in the strong sunlight of a hospital yard, I might have come away from Haiti interested but doubtful. But I saw this case of Felicia Felix-Mentor which was vouched for by the highest authority. So I know that there are Zombies in Haiti. People have been called back from the dead." In addition to her own witness and gaze, she enlists the witness of Haitian peasants, voodoo priests, and medical experts, who argue that zombification may be a "semblance of death induced by some drug known to a few" and brought from Africa.[65]

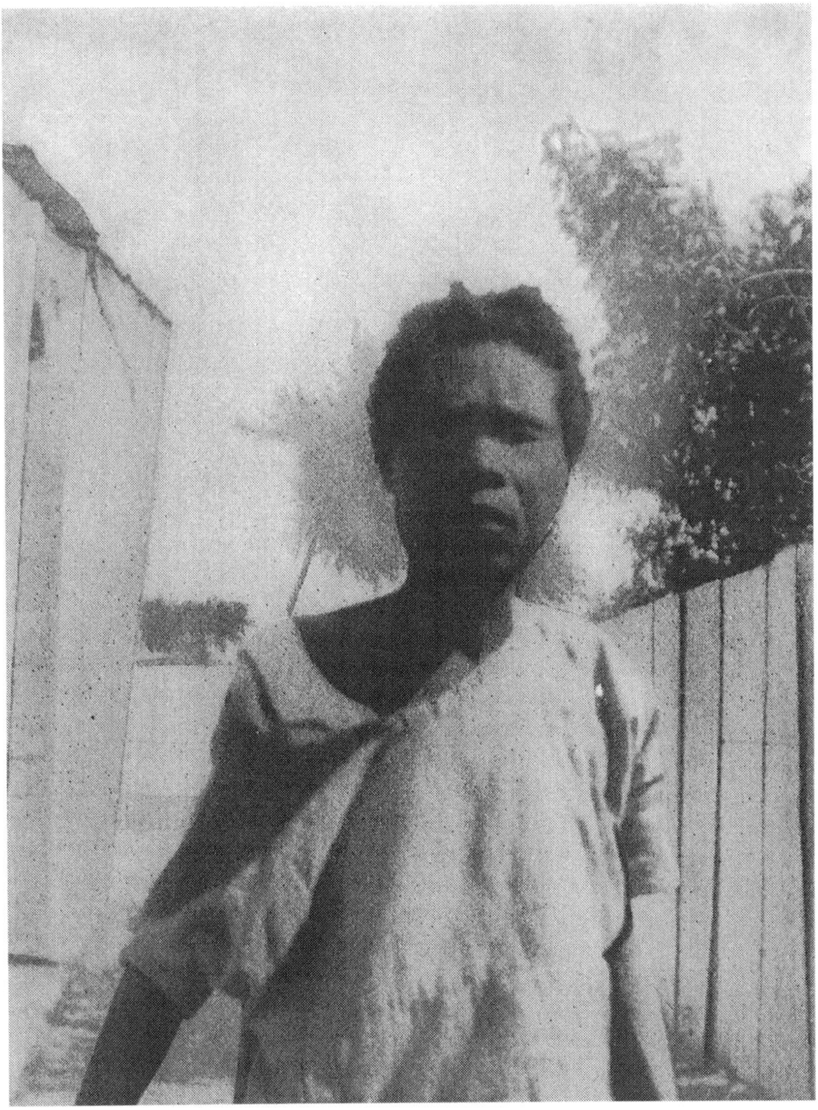

FIGURE 3. "Felicia Felix-Mentor, The Zombie." Source: Zora Neale Hurston, *Tell My Horse* (1938).

As Hurston delves into this question further, she also acquires dangerous knowledge, including the names of evil houngans who may be connected with the deaths of those who become Zombies. She is warned by a friend that she "should not go around alone picking acquaintances with these houngans. You are liable to get involved in something that is not good," and a Dr. Legros tells her that she might find herself "involved in . . . something from which [she] could not extricate [herself] alive."[66] By mentioning the potential dangers attending her quest for knowledge, Hurston accentuates the physical lengths to which she will go to collect valid cultural information, observing that if you "stay in Haiti long enough and really mingle with the people, the time will come when you hear secret societies mentioned." A well-known Port-au-Prince physician tells her that many white writers who spend just a little time in Haiti think that voodoo and the practices of the secret societies are one and the same, but, he says to Hurston, "if you are friendly to Haiti as you say you are, you must speak the truth to the world."[67] The physician gives her a mandate to learn and speak the truth in contrast to the limited information about Haiti provided by white writers and anthropologists.

Hurston considers her approach superior to that of colleagues like Herskovits, who also mentions secret societies but without apparent personal experience. In a July 30, 1936, letter to Herskovits from the Maroon settlement of Accompong Town, Jamaica, and in reference to the more accessible Maroon ceremonies that he likely witnessed, she insists that one has "not seen Maroon ceremony" unless he or she has witnessed the major ceremony held in August, which she plans to attend. Writing to Moe from Port-au-Prince on September 24, 1936, Hurston claims that neither Herskovits nor Dunham stayed in Accompong long enough "to find out about what was really going on" (according to Hurston, Herskovits was there for only eight days).[68] In *Tell My Horse,* Hurston implies that the same could be said of Herskovits's claims about human sacrifice among secret societies. Emphasizing her own determination to penetrate the culture deeply enough to achieve firsthand knowledge, she asks, "How can I say these things until I am very sure?" and then states that she later "found what [Herskovits's informants] said to be true" about the practice of human sacrifice in some of the secret societies.[69] Hurston emphasizes the authority of her first-person methods and the information that she gathers through these methods, underscored by the physical danger she risks to acquire it.[70]

As she notes elsewhere in the text, some ceremonies require one to "participate in [the ceremony] to fully appreciate it," and in her descriptions of one secret society, the Sect Rouge, she seems to indicate that she witnessed firsthand a meeting of the society on a bridge across the lake at Mher.

Although she draws on passages from other sources to describe the event (such as quotes from a book by Moreau de Saint-Méry describing the cannibalizing of babies), her description implies that she was present. She writes that the ceremony is "an awful sight to the late traveller! The bridge covered with candles, the brilliantly costumed figures, themselves bearing multiple candles and the little coffin that is their object of worship. . . . This is how a meeting was held." Furthermore, her claim that she eventually corroborates what her sources have told her about secret societies,[71] and, after describing the dire fate of those who share such secrets, her representation of the Sect Rouge meeting as a firsthand account, suggest the added risks she may have taken to acquire firsthand knowledge and emphasize both her superior authority as a physically present participant and the dangerous physical work of collecting cultural knowledge.

The slippage here between participant and observer, one that is sometimes not clearly delineated, as we have seen, is characteristic of Hurston's work. As Wendy Dutton notes of Hurston's writing about voodoo, "her confusion about the appropriate mode of telling is almost palpable in her writing."[72] Hurston blurs these lines between participant and observer in other work such as "Hoodoo in America" (1931) and *Mules and Men* (1935), where, as Dorothea Fischer-Hornung has argued, Hurston personalizes her descriptions of folk belief (through the creation of her protagonist "Zora"), contrasting the "objective ethnographic description" with "the subjective experience of abject horror in which personal boundaries of revulsion and fear are crossed," and thus "describing in great detail the slippery liminality between participant and observer."[73] Alasdair Pettinger also observes how Hurston "repeatedly undercuts the rhetoric of the "firsthand" through "the curiously 'quoted' feel" of the text. Through Hurston's use of indirect speech and paraphrase, Pettinger argues, "the boundary between quotation, or mere belief, and the expected, arbitrating voice of the omniscient narrator is blurred" in *Tell My Horse,* "making the very existence of this voice uncertain."[74] Even if it is not always clear whether or not Hurston saw or participated in some of the ceremonies she writes about, I read her personalized representation of the ceremonies in the travel narrative and her tendency to transgress boundaries of genre and ethnographic method as deliberate strategies she uses to assert authority in the text as a witness and traveler.

Two final aspects of the text further illustrate this representation of authority, especially as it is connected to her physically mobile black female body. First, near the end of the text, she describes how individuals are possessed by Papa Guédé, a god of the Haitian peasants. A possession is indicated when the person, known as the "horse," is mounted by the spirit and utters the phrase "Parlay cheval ou" (Tell my horse]. The horse then channels the spirit of Guédé, saying and doing that which is "true," that which the peasants themselves, uninhibited, would like to say and do. Hurston observes that while some people may genuinely be possessed, many feign possession "as a blind for self expression" and "in order to express their resentment general and particular." Similarly, Hurston believes that her mouth and body act as channels for transmitting the truth about Haiti, as she implies throughout the text and, most notably, when she reports her conversation with the Port-au-Prince physician who asks her to tell the truth about the distinctions between voodoo and Haitian secret societies.[75] Ultimately, her text, aptly titled *Tell My Horse,* becomes in this case the possessed "horse," embodiment of the spirit of Guédé and the vehicle through which Hurston can express the truth. While the spirit of Guédé prefers the uninhibited truth, however, Hurston has been somewhat more judicious in selecting and omitting cultural information in order to navigate particular gendered and scholarly terrains. The fact that she cannot speak utterly unencumbered suggests some of the constraints placed on her work and her voice, but she downplays these constraints through her emphasis on the physical mobility and cultural access she enjoys.

Second, she ends with a folktale that she hears from Dr. Reser, a white man who has taken up residence in Haiti and who is often sought out by foreign visitors as a source of information about the island. She spends time on his porch listening to his opinions about Haiti, folklore, religion, science, and travel. Linking her mobility to her acquisition of cultural knowledge, and emphasizing her self-sufficient power to perform cultural work, Hurston points out that unlike most other visitors to Haiti, "I never went to him for the information that I had come to Haiti to seek . . . because I consider myself amply equipped to go out in the field and get it myself." In the spirit of Guédé, she says that she is breaking a promise by writing about him in her text.[76] This lapse in protocol further emphasizes her authority to speak, move, and transgress boundaries freely as a black female traveler and ethnographer. Furthermore, by ending her text with the folktale "God and the Pintards," which she hears from Reser, she also appropriates its message for her own work of cultural transmission and preservation. The tale recounts God's sending the angels Michael, Gabriel, and Peter to kill the unruly pintards (or guinea fowls) that are eating up his rice fields. When each in turn fails, God himself comes down to the rice fields, but he, like his angels, is so taken by the pintards' music and laughter that he cannot kill them and instead commissions them to take these gifts to his newly created world. Like the figure of God in the tale, Hurston comes to Haiti to see for herself, and like the pintards, she receives a commission, both personal and professional, to take what she receives there and share her gifts, words, and knowledge with the rest of the world.

This concluding folktale of *Tell My Horse* establishes connections between travel and the transmission of cultural knowledge that Hurston would revisit in her 1938–39 Florida guidebook entries, written under the auspices of the Federal Writers' Project. Departing from typical guidebook fare in her entry "Eatonville When You Look at It," Hurston leads would-be visitors through her supposed birthplace on a tour that identifies the major landmarks (houses, stores, and corners) in terms of their association with the bodies and identities of specific residents, including herself: "After [Joe Clark's] shop you come to the Widow Dash's orange grove, her screened porch, 'double hips,' and her new husband. Way down the end of the road to the right is Claude Mann's filling station and beyond that the last home in Eatonville, the big barn on the lake that is lived in by Zora Hurston." Hurston implies that beyond what one can see from the main street, the real life of the town is found in the "back streets" filled with old houses "made out of the town's first dreams" or in the public school yards and playground "that Howard Miller always looks after though he can scarcely read and write."[77] Recalling the role that Hurston adopts through the retelling of the tale of God and the pintards in *Tell My Horse,* in the Florida guidebook entries she assumes the position of expert witness and the transmitter or voice of specialized insider knowledge about the culture, which she has acquired through firsthand experience.

Referring to the guidebooks as "New Negro Americana," Ulysses Lee writes with enthusiasm in *Opportunity* about the way the Federal Writers' Project American Guide Series "often contain more facts about Negroes than can be found in any other single place,"[78] though he does complain about the tendency, as seen in the New Orleans guide, to focus on the Old South, a complaint that Locke also shares.[79] Lee sees the New Orleans book as "more than a guide; it is an interpretation" of the black influence on the city, but he also writes that "a premium is placed upon the picturesque, the gay, and the folksy," while social problems in New Orleans and elsewhere are glossed over. In the Mississippi guide, he notes, "whatever phases of the state's life happen not to fit the ordained pattern are shorn, ignored, or garnished until they emerge as polished props in a pastoral setting."[80] While Lee and Locke might consider Hurston's entries similarly folksy or idealized, these pieces underscore the close connection between physical bodies and cultural authority in her travel writing. In Hurston's guidebook entries, physical location is embodied in the people who experience and have knowledge about these spaces and who, through their bodies and voices, transmit cultural knowledge about these spaces to others. Hurston claims a similarly embodied authority to preserve and transmit her cultural knowledge of Haiti and Jamaica.

Hurston's acts of travel and travel writing emphasize the increased mobility of early twentieth-century African Americans and allow her to reimagine black female mobility and subjectivity in *Tell My Horse*. By resisting the erasure of her body in her travels and travel text, indeed by highlighting the physical dimensions of her travel experience, Hurston asserts her own cultural authority and provides a model for other African Americans, particularly women, of how one might successfully preserve and transmit cultural knowledge and thus counter the narratives of diminished subjectivity and mobility propagated by both the experience and subsequent critical readings of the Middle Passage and its legacies. Ultimately, Hurston's narrative highlights important features of the black travel text: the emphasis on cultural work (over sightseeing or tourism), the trope of the body in representing issues of mobility and identity, and the high stakes of such work for African Americans and particularly African American women. Bartkowski argues that the ambivalent rhetoric in *Tell My Horse* creates a tension between Hurston's roles as researcher and traveler.[81] I would suggest that we view this not as a tension but as an example of the cultural dissonances drawing our attention to the representation of travel *as* cultural work in the writing of Hurston and other African American travelers during the Jim Crow era.

EPILOGUE

The work of African American travel writers during the Jim Crow era is distinctive for its cultural dissonances, often represented as oscillations between the body and the gaze, conservatism and progressive critique, stasis and mobility, fact and stereotype, or eyewitness observation and recirculated commentary. Such oscillations are examined through an array of identity positions ranging between layperson and professional, observer and participant, servant and explorer, or conciliator and agitator. As they negotiate the period's social constraints through the themes and formal conventions of the travel narrative, African American travel writers expand our understanding of the relationship of mobility to various forms of resistance, authority, and identity during the age of Jim Crow.

These narratives are distinctive for the diverse and often covert strategies through which African American travelers exert resistance and claim authority in an atmosphere hostile to such expressions of black identity and power. The sometimes veiled critique of the African American travel narrative recalls Richard Wright's assertion, in "The Ethics of Living Jim Crow" (1937), that his Jim Crow experience taught him "to lie, to steal, to dissemble[,] . . . [and] to play that dual role which every Negro must play if he wants to eat and live."[1] Brian Norman and Piper Kendrix Williams argue that Wright's essay points to the narrative strategies ("to lie, to steal, to dissemble") that black writers developed to represent the truth of their segregation experiences.[2]

African American travel writers also engage in this work of dissembling, as in Matthew Henson's veiled critique of Robert Peary, Jessie Redmon Fauset's embedding of her cultural critique within descriptions of the mundane, or Zora Neale Hurston's dialectic of gender performance and professional authority. Sometimes travel writers' narrative responses to Jim Crow are problematic and even appear to be contradictory, as in Booker T. Washington's conciliatory approach to broader racial progress, Henson's use of imperialistic and racist rhetoric to assert his authority as an explorer, Fauset's reversion to racist and Orientalist stereotype to enact her cultural critique, or Hurston's imposition of U.S. racial and gender politics on her Caribbean subjects. But African American travel writers' challenge to oppressive ideology can also be direct and unflinching, as in Ida B. Wells's exposure and critique of the rape myth or Hurston's rejection of gender norms that place women in passive roles.

The travel narrative offers an important and unique form in which writers can enlist a variety of narrative strategies to resist Jim Crow. Indeed, when coupled with the issues of mobility and identity so central to travel writing, these strategies become powerful tools for challenging the social and physical violence and oppression of Jim Crow policy. While notions of racial uplift and mobility have important metaphorical and cultural meanings during the period, the fact that the travel narrative is concerned with actual physical mobility allows black travel writers to craft particularly forceful expressions of African American identity and resistance.

Threats to black mobility have not disappeared with the ending of Jim Crow. The cultural work of these travel narratives and what they teach us about African American resistance and cultural authority is as important today as it was during their moment of publication. In May 2014, the Civil Rights Project at UCLA issued a report on the sixtieth anniversary of *Brown v. Board of Education,* noting that while school segregation in the South has not returned to pre-*Brown* levels, the region has lost all of the progress on the issue that was made from the mid-1960s until the late 1980s. The report also discusses dramatic increases in school segregation for Latino students in the western United States, noting that black and Latino students often attend the same underserved schools, in which a large majority of the students are of a lower socioeconomic status.[3]

Furthermore, the ongoing economic and social consequences in urban and suburban neighborhoods caused by the redlining practices of financial institutions beginning in the 1930s,[4] and conversations about racial profiling and violence prompted by the shooting of Michael Brown, Trayvon Martin, and similar cases, call our collective attention to ongoing threats to African American mobility and the unfinished work of equality in the United States. Writing of the Martin case, Martha J. Cutter notes that the FBI's Supplementary Homicide Reports from 1980–2010 reveal that "whites are ten times more likely to be able to kill a black stranger with impunity in the name of 'self-defense' than if these racial roles are reversed. We might think of differential justice systems as a product of the past and of Jim Crow, but they are with us now, in the present moment."[5] Reports of such imbalances fill our news feeds and proliferate through social media even as some argue that the United States has entered a post-racial era.

The African American travel narrative in the age of Jim Crow is significant, then, not only for how it represents black mobility during the period but also for how it illuminates continuing threats to such mobility. In light of ongoing inequities in racial justice, Ida B. Wells's argument about racial violence is unnervingly prescient: "If the same zeal to excuse and conceal the facts were exercised to put a stop to these lynchings, there would be no need for me to relate nor for the . . . press to give ear to these tales of barbarity."[6] There has been a negligible reduction in the excusing and concealing of racial injustice in U.S. public discourse since Wells undertook her antilynching tours; in fact, we might argue that the rhetoric against racial justice has increased in the past decade or so. Thus the "need . . . to relate" and "give ear to" such injustice is as great as ever. The travel narratives discussed in this volume provide models for the cultural work and narrative strategies through which writers might resist the continuing legacies of Jim Crow and assert African American authority and identity.

NOTES

INTRODUCTION

1. Ida B. Wells, *Crusade for Justice: The Autobiography of Ida B. Wells,* ed. Alfreda M. Duster (Chicago: University of Chicago Press, 1970), 44.
2. Patricia A. Schechter, "Unsettled Business: Ida B. Wells against Lynching, or, How Antilynching Got Its Gender," in *Under Sentence of Death: Lynching in the South,* ed. W. Fitzhugh Brundage (Chapel Hill: University of North Carolina Press, 1997), 305.
3. Wells, *Crusade for Justice,* 178.
4. Zora Neale Hurston, *Tell My Horse* (Philadelphia: Lippincott, 1938), 35.
5. *Zora Neale Hurston: A Life in Letters,* ed. Carla Kaplan (New York: Doubleday, 2002), 376.
6. Hurston uses the term "voodoo" to refer to the Vodun religion in *Tell My Horse,* and I use this same term in my discussion of her text.
7. Ida B. Wells-Barnett, *Southern Horrors* (1892) and *A Red Record* (1895), in *On Lynchings: Ida B. Wells-Barnett,* ed. Patricia Hill Collins (Amherst, N.Y.: Humanity Books, 2002), 25–54, 55–151.
8. A number of African American writers traveled to Europe during this time. William A. Shack also notes the many black musicians who traveled to the Montmartre district of Paris to perform in the early twentieth century (*Harlem in Montmartre: A Paris Jazz Story between the Great Wars* [Berkeley: University of California Press, 2001]).
9. W. E. B Du Bois, "Opinion of W. E. B. Du Bois," *The Crisis,* March 1921, 197.
10. Mary Louise Pratt, *Imperial Eyes: Travel Writing and Enculturation,* 2nd ed. (New York: Routledge, 2008).
11. For a discussion of similar issues in relation to women writers and Harlem Renaissance periodization, see Venetria K. Patton and Maureen Honey, introduction to *Double-Take: A Revisionist Harlem Renaissance Anthology,* ed. Venetria K. Patton and Maureen Honey (New Brunswick: Rutgers University Press, 2001), xix–xxxix. Barbara McCaskill and Caroline Gebhard note that conventional approaches to the time span

from the end of Reconstruction to the end of World War I view the period as the "nadir" of African American thought and culture. Though these decades were filled with "increased violence and de facto racial segregation," McCaskill and Gebhard also note that their reappraisal of this "post-bellum, Pre-Harlem" period reveals how it was "a crucial stage in African American cultural and literary history and a period of high aesthetic experimentation and political dynamism," without which the Harlem Renaissance would not have been possible (introduction to *Post-Bellum, Pre-Harlem: African American Literature and Culture, 1877–1919,* ed. Barbara McCaskill and Caroline Gebhard [New York: New York University Press, 2006], 1, 2, 4). As my own book demonstrates, important work was also being done by African American writers during this time in the genre of the travel narrative.

12. Stephen Greenblatt, "Resonance and Wonder," *Bulletin of the Academy of Arts and Sciences* 43, no. 4 (1990): 19.
13. Stephen Greenblatt, "Culture," in *Critical Terms for Literary Study,* 2nd ed., ed. Frank Lentricchia and Thomas McLaughlin (Chicago: University of Chicago Press, 1995), 228, 229.
14. Heather Russell, *Legba's Crossing: Narratology in the African Atlantic* (Athens: University of Georgia Press, 2009), 3.
15. Frances Bartkowski, *Travelers, Immigrants, Inmates: Essays in Estrangement* (Minneapolis: University of Minnesota Press, 1995), 101.
16. Critics noting the genre's heterogeneity include Peter Hulme and Tim Youngs (introduction to *The Cambridge Companion to Travel Writing,* ed. Peter Hulme and Tim Youngs [New York: Cambridge University Press, 2002], 10–11); Dennis Porter (*Haunted Journeys: Desire and Transgression in European Travel Writing* [Princeton: Princeton University Press, 1991], 19); and John Zilcosky ("Writing Travel," in *Writing Travel: The Poetics and Politics of the Modern Journey,* ed. John Zilcosky [Toronto: University of Toronto Press, 2008], 7–8).
17. Booker T. Washington, *The Man Farthest Down: A Record of Observation and Study in Europe* (Garden City, N.Y.: Doubleday, 1912).
18. The particular effects of the slave trade and its aftermath on American identity have been examined at length by critics such as James Olney ("'I Was Born': Slave Narratives, Their Status as Autobiography and as Literature," *Callaloo* 20 [Winter 1984]: 46–73); Valerie Smith (*Self-Discovery and Authority in Afro-American Narrative* [Cambridge: Harvard University Press, 1987]); William L. Andrews (introduction to *African American Autobiography: A Collection of Critical Essays,* ed. William L. Andrews [Englewood Cliffs, N.J.: Prentice Hall, 1993], 1–25); and Farah Jasmine Griffin (*"Who Set You Flowin'?" The African-American Migration Narrative* [New York: Oxford University Press, 1995]).
19. Griffin, *"Who Set You Flowin'?,"* 3, 16.
20. Hazel Carby, "The Politics of Fiction, Anthropology, and the Folk: Zora Neale Hurston," in *History and Memory in African-American Culture,* ed. Geneviève Fabre and Robert O'Meally (New York: Oxford University Press, 1994), 31, 40.
21. Eve E. Dunbar, *Black Regions of the Imagination: African American Writers between the Nation and the World* (Philadelphia: Temple University Press, 2013), 21, 30–31.
22. Sidonie Smith, *Moving Lives: Twentieth-Century Women's Travel Writing* (Minneapolis: University of Minnesota Press, 2001), xii.
23. Farah J. Griffin and Cheryl J. Fish, introduction to *A Stranger in the Village: Two Centu-*

ries of African-American Travel Writing, ed. Farah J. Griffin and Cheryl J. Fish (Boston: Beacon Press, 1998), xiv.

24. Paul Gilroy, *The Black Atlantic: Modernity and Double Consciousness* (Cambridge: Harvard University Press, 1993). Recent studies have expanded the scope of Gilroy's paradigm to include Indian, Mediterranean, or intra-African diasporas (for example, Paul Tiyambe Zeleza, "Rewriting the African Diaspora: Beyond the Black Atlantic," *African Affairs* 104, no. 414 [2005]: 35–68). Scholarship that extends Gilroy's examination of the black Atlantic as an influence on the genealogies of modernity and globalism includes Maria Diedrich, Henry Louis Gates Jr., and Carl Pedersen, eds., *Black Imagination and the Middle Passage* (New York: Oxford University Press, 1999); James Walvin, *Making the Black Atlantic: Britain and the African Diaspora* (London: Cassell, 2000); and Peter Linebaugh and Marcus Rediker's early history *The Many-Headed Hydra: Sailors, Slaves, Commoners, and the Hidden History of the Revolutionary Atlantic* (Boston: Beacon Press, 2000). Brent Hayes Edwards, in *The Practice of Diaspora: Literature, Translation, and the Rise of Black Internationalism* (Cambridge: Harvard University Press, 2003), emphasizes the global dimensions of black travel in the early twentieth century in relation to the multiple translation practices during the period. In *At Home in Diaspora: Black International Writing* (Minneapolis: University of Minnesota Press, 2005), Wendy W. Walters complicates the conventional opposition between home and mobility in the work of black international writers during this period, and Dunbar explores links between African American writers' international experiences and their construction of black experience in the United States in *Black Regions of the Imagination* (2013). Russell in *Legba's Crossing* (2009) conducts a narratological analysis of black texts that disrupt prescriptive Euro-American literary conventions, though she does not focus on the genre of the travel narrative, and Keith Cartwright emphasizes the "modes of Afro-creole agency" that shaped the modernity of the Caribbean and Deep South in *Sacral Grooves, Limbo Gateways: Travels in Deep Southern Time, Circum-Caribbean Space, Afro-Creole Authority* (Athens: University of Georgia Press, 2013), 5.
25. Hulme and Youngs, introduction, 10.
26. Mary Baine Campbell, "Travel Writing and Its Theory," in Hulme and Youngs, *Cambridge Companion to Travel Writing,* 262; Alasdair Pettinger, introduction to *Always Elsewhere: Travels of the Black Atlantic,* ed. Alasdair Pettinger (London: Cassell, 1998), xii.
27. Paul Smethurst, introduction to *Travel Writing, Form, and Empire: The Poetics and Politics of Mobility,* ed. Julia Kuehn and Paul Smethurst (New York: Routledge, 2009), 1, 2, 7.
28. Zilcosky, "Writing Travel," 5.
29. Smethurst, introduction, 7.
30. Zilcosky, "Writing Travel," 8, 9.
31. Jan Borm, "Defining Travel: On the Travel Book, Travel Writing and Terminology," in *Perspectives on Travel Writing,* ed. Glen Hooper and Tim Youngs (London: Ashgate, 2004), 13; Jan Borm, "*In-Betweeners*? On the Travel Book and Ethnographies," *Studies In Travel Writing* 4, no. 1 (2000): 78.
32. Alfred Bendixen and Judith Hamera, introduction to *The Cambridge Companion to American Travel Writing,* ed. Alfred Bendixen and Judith Hamera (Cambridge: Cambridge University Press, 2009), 2, 3.
33. Philip Gould, "Beginnings: The Origins of American Travel Writing," ibid., 13; Wayne

Franklin, *Discoverers, Explorers, Settlers: The Diligent Writers of Early America* (Chicago: University of Chicago Press, 1979), 21.

34. Variations of these stories are recorded in Langston Hughes and Arna Bontemps's edited collection *The Book of Negro Folklore* (New York: Dodd, Mead, 1958) and in the Georgia Writers' Project's *Drums and Shadows: Survival Studies Among the Georgia Coastal Negroes* (Athens: University of Georgia Press, 1940).
35. Virginia Whatley Smith, "African American Travel Literature," in Bendixen and Hamera, *Cambridge Companion to American Travel Writing,* 198.
36. Bendixen and Hamera, introduction, 5, 6.
37. Ibid., 6–7.
38. Wells, *Crusade for Justice,* 174.
39. Hurston, *Tell My Horse,* 17, 18.
40. Booker T. Washington, introduction to *A Negro Explorer at the North Pole* (1912), by Matthew Henson (Montpelier, Vt.: Invisible Cities Press, 2001), xxxiii.
41. Jessie Redmon Fauset, "Dark Algiers the White: Part I," *The Crisis,* April 1925, 255–58; "Dark Algiers the White: Part II," *The Crisis,* May 1925, 16–20; "This Way to the Flea Market," *The Crisis,* February 1925, 161–63; and "Yarrow Revisited," *The Crisis,* January 1925, 109.
42. Deborah McDowell, "Introduction: Regulating Midwives," in *Plum Bun: A Novel without a Moral* (1929), by Jessie Redmon Fauset (Boston: Beacon Press, 1990), xii; Sterling Brown, *Negro Poetry and Drama* and *The Negro in American Fiction* (1937; New York: Atheneum, 1968), 142; Robert Bone, *The Negro Novel in America* (New Haven: Yale University Press, 1965), 101.
43. Evelyn Brooks Higginbotham, *Righteous Discontent: The Women's Movement in the Black Baptist Church, 1880–1920* (Cambridge: Harvard University Press, 1993), 187.
44. Jessie Redmon Fauset, "Sunday Afternoon," *The Crisis,* February 1922, 162–64. I am indebted to Amy Rupiper Taggart, who noted this juxtaposition in Fauset's work and examined her participation in the rhetoric of respectability in a presentation at the 2011 Feminisms and Rhetorics conference, "The Axis of Agency and Social Control: Jessie Fauset's Rhetorical Space and Rhetoric of Respectability." Rupiper Taggart, however, does not examine this phenomenon in Fauset's travel essays.
45. Ronald E. Martin, *The Languages of Difference: American Writers and Anthropologists Reconfigure the Primitive, 1878–1940* (Newark: University of Delaware Press, 2005), 234–63; Robert E. Hemenway, *Zora Neale Hurston: A Literary Biography* (Urbana: University of Illinois Press, 1977), 213.

1. EMBODYING SEGREGATION

1. Ida B. Wells, *Crusade for Justice: The Autobiography of Ida B. Wells,* ed. Alfreda M. Duster (Chicago: University of Chicago Press, 1970), 113.
2. Alsadair Pettinger, "At Sea—Coloured Passenger," in *Sea Changes: Historicizing the Ocean,* ed. Bernhard Klein and Gesa Mackenthun (New York: Routledge, 2004), 153–54.
3. Wells, *Crusade for Justice,* 4.
4. Olaudah Equiano, *The Interesting Narrative of the Life of Olaudah Equiano, or Gustavas Vassa, the African. Written by Himself* (1789; New York: W. Durrell, 1791); Mary Seacole, *Wonderful Adventures of Mrs. Seacole in Many Lands* (London: James Blackwood, 1857);

Frederick Douglass, "Letter from Scotland" (1846) and "A Month in Egypt" (1886–87), in *Always Elsewhere: Travels of the Black Atlantic,* ed. Alasdair Pettinger (London: Cassell, 1998), 95–97, 209–14; A. B. C. Merriman-Labor, *Britons through Negro Spectacles; or, A Negro on Britons. With a Description of London* (London: Imperial and Foreign Company, 1909); Matthew Alexander Henson, *A Negro Explorer at the North Pole* (New York: F. A. Stokes, 1912).

5. Wells, *Crusade for Justice,* 169; all references to Wells's *Inter-Ocean* column are from this source, in which the articles are reprinted.
6. Hélène Christol, "The African American Concept of the Fantastic as Middle Passage," in *Black Imagination and the Middle Passage,* ed. Maria Diedrich, Henry Louis Gates Jr., and Carl Pedersen (New York: Oxford University Press, 1999), 164.
7. Paul Gilroy, *The Black Atlantic: Modernity and Double Consciousness* (Cambridge: Harvard University Press, 1993), 71.
8. Peter Linebaugh and Marcus Rediker, *The Many-Headed Hydra: Sailors, Slaves, Commoners, and the Hidden History of the Revolutionary Atlantic* (Boston: Beacon Press, 2000), 327.
9. Hortense J. Spillers, "Mama's Baby, Papa's Maybe: An American Grammar Book," *Diacritics* 17, no. 2 (1987): 72.
10. Wells, *Crusade for Justice,* 128, 131.
11. Gilroy, *The Black Atlantic,* 19.
12. Wells, *Crusade for Justice,* 135.
13. Gilroy, *The Black Atlantic,* 19.
14. Carolyn L. Karcher, "Ida B. Wells and Her Allies against Lynching: A Transnational Perspective," *Comparative American Studies* 3, no. 2 (2005): 135.
15. Wells, *Crusade for Justice,* 133, 135, 136.
16. Ibid., 153, 143–45, 171–74.
17. Booker T. Washington, *The Man Farthest Down: A Record of Observation and Study in Europe* (Garden City, N.Y.: Doubleday, Page, 1912), 10, 13.
18. Wells, *Crusade for Justice,* 178.
19. Wells quoted in *The Booker T. Washington Papers,* ed. Louis R. Harlan, vol. 3 (Urbana: University of Illinois Press, 1974), 108.
20. Wells, *Crusade for Justice,* 41.
21. Wells quoted in *Booker T. Washington Papers,* 3:108.
22. Wells, *Crusade for Justice,* 41.
23. Ibid., 265.
24. Patricia A. Schechter, *Ida B. Wells-Barnett and American Reform, 1880–1930* (Chapel Hill: University of North Carolina Press, 2001), 130.
25. Wells, *Crusade for Justice,* 331.
26. Quoted in Schechter, *Ida B. Wells-Barnett,* 131.
27. Ibid., 108, 109.
28. Ibid., 61–62, 65–66.
29. Ida B. Wells, *Southern Horrors* (1892), in *On Lynchings: Ida B. Wells-Barnett,* ed. Patricia Hill Collins (Amherst, N.Y.: Humanity Books, 2002), 31.
30. Wells, *Crusade for Justice,* 62–63, 69, 64, 71.
31. Ibid., 135, 152, 155.
32. Gail Bederman, *Manliness and Civilization: A Cultural History of Gender and Race in the United States, 1880–1917* (Chicago: University of Chicago Press, 1995), 46.

33. Wells, *Crusade for Justice,* 31, 147, 150.
34. Patricia A. Schechter, "Unsettled Business: Ida B. Wells against Lynching, or, How Anti-lynching Got Its Gender," in *Under Sentence of Death: Lynching in the South,* ed. W. Fitzhugh Brundage (Chapel Hill: University of North Carolina Press, 1997), 292, 296, 297–98, 301. In her essay on the Anita Hill–Clarence Thomas hearings, Elsa Barkley Brown explores the ways in which we continue to elide the lynching of black women ("Imaging Lynching: African American Women, Communities of Struggle, and Collective Memory," in *African American Women Speak Out on Anita Hill–Clarence Thomas,* ed. Geneva Smitherman [Detroit: Wayne State University Press, 1995], 102).
35. Schechter, *Ida B. Wells-Barnett,* 114.
36. Nicole King, "'A Colored Woman in Another Country Pleading for Justice in Her Own': Ida B. Wells in Great Britain," in *Black Victorians/Black Victoriana,* ed. Gretchen Holbrook Gerzina (New Brunswick: Rutgers University Press, 2003), 88–109, quotation on 95.
37. King, in "'A Colored Woman in Another Country,'" and Schechter, in *Ida B. Wells-Barnett,* also discuss Wells's performative identity but not in the context of travel and travel writing.
38. Linda O. McMurry, *To Keep the Waters Troubled: The Life of Ida B. Wells* (New York: Oxford University Press, 1998), 169.
39. Schechter, "Unsettled Business," 307–9.
40. Bederman, *Manliness and Civilization,* 63.
41. Schechter, "Unsettled Business," 305.
42. Wells, *Crusade for Justice,* 44.
43. Ida B. Wells, *The Memphis Diary of Ida B. Wells,* ed. Miriam DeCosta-Willis (Boston: Beacon Press, 1995), 77–79, 189.
44. King, "'A Colored Woman in Another Country,'" 92.
45. Wells, *Crusade for Justice,* 113.
46. For an analysis of Wells's embodiment in relation to U.S. citizenship, see Alison Piepmeier, *Out in Public: Configurations of Women's Bodies in Nineteenth-Century America* (Chapel Hill: University of North Carolina Press, 2004).
47. Schechter, "Unsettled Business," 302.
48. Marguerite Helmers and Tilar J. Mazzeo, "Introduction: Travel and the Body," *Journal of Narrative Theory* 35, no. 3 (2005): 267, 268.
49. Mary Louise Pratt, *Imperial Eyes: Travel Writing and Transculturation,* 2nd ed. (New York: Routledge, 2008).
50. Radhika Mohanram, *Black Body: Women, Colonialism, and Space* (Minneapolis: University of Minnesota Press, 1999), 16.
51. Edward Said, *Orientalism* (New York: Pantheon, 1978).
52. Lila M. Harper, *Solitary Travelers: Nineteenth-Century Women's Travel Narratives and the Scientific Vocation* (Madison, N.J.: Farleigh Dickinson University Press, 2001); Sara Mills, *Discourses of Difference: An Analysis of Women's Travel Writing and Colonialism* (New York: Routledge, 1991).
53. Helmers and Mazzeo, "Introduction," 270.
54. Wells, *Crusade for Justice,* 159, 71.
55. Ibid., 115–18. Wells resented the fair's belated sponsorship of a "Negro Day" and signaled her displeasure with Douglass's decision to speak at the event by boycotting his speech.

After reading about the speech in the papers the next day, however, she "went straight out to the fair and begged his pardon for presuming in [her] youth and inexperience to criticize him for an effort which had done more to bring our cause to the attention of the American people than anything else which had happened during the fair" (119).

56. Wells, ibid., 163–64, emphasis added.
57. Farah J. Griffin and Cheryl J. Fish, introduction to *A Stranger in the Village: Two Centuries of African-American Travel Writing,* ed. Farah J. Griffin and Cheryl J. Fish (Boston: Beacon Press, 1998), xiv–xv.
58. Gilroy, *The Black Atlantic,* 186.
59. W. E. B. Du Bois, *The Souls of Black Folk* (1903), in *Three Negro Classics* (New York: Avon, 1965), 215.
60. Karcher, "Ida B. Wells and Her Allies," 141, 142, 145, 144.
61. Schechter, *Ida B. Wells-Barnett,* 24.
62. Wells, *Crusade for Justice,* 214, 212.
63. Schecter, *Ida B. Wells-Barnett,* 105 (emphasis added), 25.
64. Schecter, "Unsettled Business," 295.
65. Robyn Wiegman, *American Anatomies: Theorizing Race and Gender* (Durham: Duke University Press, 1995), 84–85.
66. Wells, *Crusade for Justice,* 174, 154.
67. J. Hector St. John de Crèvecoeur, *Letters from an American Farmer* (1782; New York: Fox, Duffield, 1904); Harriet A. Jacobs, *Incidents in the Life of a Slave Girl* (1861), ed. Jean Fagan Yellin (Cambridge: Harvard University Press, 1987).
68. Spillers, "Mama's Baby, Papa's Maybe," 65.
69. Gilroy, *The Black Atlantic,* 4.
70. Schechter, *Ida B. Wells-Barnett,* 84.
71. Stuart Hall, "Minimal Selves," in *Black British Cultural Studies: A Reader,* ed. Houston A. Baker Jr., Manthia Diawara, and Ruth H. Lindeborg (Chicago: University of Chicago Press, 1996), 115.
72. Spillers, "Mama's Baby, Papa's Maybe," 80.
73. Wells, *Crusade for Justice,* 186, 187.

2. SOUTHERNIZING TRAVEL IN THE BLACK ATLANTIC

1. Farah J. Griffin and Cheryl J. Fish, introduction to *A Stranger in the Village: Two Centuries of African-American Travel Writing* (Boston: Beacon Press, 1998), xiii–xvii; Alasdair Pettinger, introduction to *Always Elsewhere: Travels of the Black Atlantic* (London: Cassell, 1998), viii–xix.
2. See St. Clair Drake's critical introduction to the 1984 edition of the text (Booker T. Washington, *The Man Farthest Down: A Record of Observation and Study in Europe* [New Brunswick N.J.: Transaction, 1984], v–lxiv); Dickson D. Bruce Jr., "Booker T. Washington's *The Man Farthest Down* and the Transformation of Race," *Mississippi Quarterly* 48, no. 2 (Spring 1995): 239–53; and Robert J. Norrell, *Up from History: The Life of Booker T. Washington* (Cambridge: Harvard University Press, 2009).
3. Houston A. Baker Jr. and Dana D. Nelson, "Preface: Violence, the Body, and 'The South,'" *American Literature* 73, no. 2 (2001): 231, 243; John Oliver Killens, *Black Man's Burden* (New York: Trident Press, 1965), 57.
4. Booker T. Washington, *Up from Slavery: An Autobiography* (New York: Doubleday, 1901).

5. Thomas Dixon Jr., *The Leopard's Spots: A Romance of the White Man's Burden, 1865–1900* (New York: Doubleday, 1902), and *The Clansman: An Historical Romance of the Ku Klux Klan* (New York: Doubleday, 1905).
6. Drake, introduction, xli–xlii, lvii–lviii.
7. Louis R. Harlan, "Booker T. Washington and the Politics of Accommodation," in *Booker T. Washington in Perspective: Essays of Louis R. Harlan,* ed. Raymond W. Smock (Jackson: University Press of Mississippi, 1988), 179; Kevern Verney, *The Art of the Possible: Booker T. Washington and Black Leadership in the United States, 1881–1925* (New York: Routledge, 2001), 65. Other scholars emphasizing the need to move beyond stereotypes about Washington include David H. Jackson Jr., who argues that Washington's "black survival strategy" challenges the notion that he was an accommodationist (*Booker T. Washington and the Struggle against White Supremacy: The Southern Educational Tours, 1908–1912* [New York: Palgrave Macmillan, 2008], 33). See also Raymond W. Smock, *Booker T. Washington: Black Leadership in the Age of Jim Crow* (Chicago: Ivan R. Dee, 2009); Norrell, *Up from History;* and the authors in *Booker T. Washington and Black Progress:* Up from Slavery *100 Years Later,* ed. W. Fitzhugh Brundage (Gainesville: University Press of Florida, 2003).
8. Paul Gilroy, *The Black Atlantic: Modernity and Double Consciousness* (Cambridge: Harvard University Press, 1993), 71.
9. John Pendleton Kennedy, *Swallow Barn; or, A Sojourn in the Old Dominion* (Philadelphia: Carey and Lea, 1832); Thomas Nelson Page, *In Ole Virginia; or, Marse Chan, and Other Stories* (New York: Scribner's, 1887).
10. Booker T. Washington, *The Man Farthest Down: A Record of Observation and Study in Europe* (Garden City, N.Y.: Doubleday, 1912), 3.
11. Washington, *Up from Slavery,* 276, 279, 280, 285.
12. Washington, *The Man Farthest Down,* 7–8, 9.
13. Pettinger, introduction, xi.
14. Washington, *The Man Farthest Down,* 9–10, 13. Washington's traveling companion and collaborator, Robert Ezra Park, later noted that Washington saw only what he wanted to see, that "when he was abroad he was not interested in the common people as I thought he would be. . . . He just wanted to get the dirt on them that was all, to discover for himself that the man farthest down in Europe had nothing on the man farthest down in the U.S." (quoted in Louis R. Harlan, *Booker T. Washington: The Wizard of Tuskegee, 1901–1915* [New York: Oxford University Press, 1983], 292). Harlan further observes that although Washington attempted to concentrate on Europe's poor, his "celebrity and his own inclination" for enjoying speaking engagements and social events "interfered" with these intentions (292).
15. Harlan, *Booker T. Washington,* 71.
16. Lyman Abbott, *Impressions of a Careless Traveler* (New York: The Outlook Company, 1907), 7.
17. Theodore Dreiser, *A Traveler at Forty* (New York: Century, 1913), 4.
18. Joseph Conrad, *Heart of Darkness* (1899), 3rd ed., ed. Robert Kimbrough (New York: Norton, 1988), 11–12.
19. Bruce, "Booker T. Washington's *The Man Farthest Down,*" 249.
20. Ida B. Wells, *Crusade for Justice: The Autobiography of Ida B. Wells,* ed. Alfreda M. Duster (Chicago: University of Chicago Press, 1970), 174, 173.
21. Houston A. Baker Jr., *Turning South Again: Re-Thinking Modernism/Re-Thinking Booker T.* (Durham: Duke University Press, 2001), 79–81.

22. James Walvin, *Making the Black Atlantic: Britain and the African Diaspora* (London: Cassell, 2000), 57.
23. Baker, *Turning South Again,* 79–81. Gilroy interprets the "return to slavery" in the work of writers such as Toni Morrison, Sherley Anne Williams, and Charles Johnson as a desire to imaginatively "restage confrontations between . . . Euro-American thought and the supposedly primitive outlook of prehistorical, cultureless, and bestial African slaves" in order "to indict those forms of rationality which have been rendered implausible by their racially exclusive character and further to explore the history of their complicity with terror systematically and rationally practised as a form of political and economic administration" (*The Black Atlantic,* 220). It would be difficult to interpret Washington's return to plantation ideology as equally subversive.
24. Washington, *The Man Farthest Down,* 127, 128, 38, 36.
25. Booker T. Washington, "Industrial Education for the Negro" (1903), in *The Negro Problem: Centennial Edition,* ed. Bernard R. Boxill (Amherst, N.Y.: Humanity, 2003), 19; Andreá N. Williams, *Dividing Lines: Class Anxiety and Postbellum Black Fiction* (Ann Arbor: University of Michigan Press, 2013), 59, 58.
26. Washington, *The Man Farthest Down,* 297, 318, 308, 161, 203, 198–200.
27. Ibid., 48, 86–104. In fact, Washington claims that the idea that farm workers could organize themselves into unions and then use such organizations to gain better wages "had never occurred" to him (91). He further discovers that "where the masses of the people are oppressed, . . . there Socialism means revolution," but in cases "where governments have shown a liberal spirit, and especially where the Socialists have had an opportunity to participate in the Government, or . . . by means of the cooperative societies . . . to do constructive work for the benefit of the masses, they have ceased to be revolutionaries" (101). Washington concludes that the best route to reform "is not by revolution, not through political machinery that tries to control and direct the individual from the outside, but by education" (102).
28. Washington, *Up from Slavery,* 52–53.
29. Washington, *The Man Farthest Down,* 39, 40, 41, 63.
30. Booker T. Washington, "Eugenics and the Negro," *New York American,* February 4, 1914, 16.
31. Baker, *Turning South Again,* 57–58.
32. Washington, *The Man Farthest Down,* 146, 154, 155, 282.
33. Ibid., 155.
34. Basil Mathews, *Booker T. Washington: Educator and Inter-racial Interpreter* (London: SCM Press, 1949), 263–64.
35. Washington, *The Man Farthest Down,* 124, 125.
36. Baker, *Turning South Again,* 81.
37. C. Vann Woodward, *Origins of the New South, 1877–1913* (Baton Rouge: Louisiana State University Press, 1971), 365.
38. Washington, *The Man Farthest Down,* 125–26.
39. Harlan, *Booker T. Washington,* 172.
40. Booker T. Washington, "Teaching Domestic Economy at Tuskegee," *Good Housekeeping,* November 1910, 623.
41. *The Tuskegee Institute News Clippings File* (microfilm; Tuskegee: Carver Research Foundation, Tuskegee Institute, 1976).
42. Baker, *Turning South Again,* 55.

43. *The Booker T. Washington Papers,* 14 vols., ed. Louis R. Harlan et al. (Urbana: University of Illinois Press, 1972–1989), 13:500, 502.
44. Ibid., 7:190, 197.
45. Ibid., 9:252, 12:81.
46. Ibid., 10:399, 380, 490.
47. Ibid., 9:64–66.
48. Ibid., 10:62.
49. Booker T. Washington, "Business Chances for the Negro," *Leslie's Weekly,* April 23, 1908, 394.
50. *Booker T. Washington Papers,* 10:66.
51. Louis R. Harlan, "Booker T. Washington and the National Negro Business League," in *Seven on Black: Reflections on the Negro Experience in America,* ed. William G. Shade and Roy C. Herrenkohl (Philadelphia: J. B. Lippincott, 1969), 84, 86.
52. Booker T. Washington, "The Negro in Business," *American Magazine,* January 1906, 340–45.
53. Review of *The Man Farthest Down, New York Times Book Review,* October 6, 1912, 552.
54. "The Platform of the Niagara Movement," *The Outlook,* September 1, 1906, 3; "The Platform of the Outlook," *The Outlook,* September 1, 1906, 4; *Booker T. Washington Papers,* 9:67.
55. Leonard D. Abbott, *Reminiscences* (Boston: Houghton Mifflin, 1915), 415; review of *The Man Farthest Down, The Outlook,* October 5, 1912, 275; Edwin Markham, review of *The Man Farthest Down, Hearst's Magazine,* January 1913, 135. Markham's most famous work was his 1899 poem "The Man with the Hoe," an indictment of society's oppression of the laborer, revealing an interest in the plight of the working poor and calling for reform. Leonard D. Abbott referred to Markham as "the Bard of Labor" ("Edwin Markham: Laureate of Labor," *Comrade* 1, no. 4 [1902]: 75).
56. *Booker T. Washington Papers,* 12:40–41. Harlan observes that Park tried to "tone down" Washington's optimism when sections of the text were serialized in *The Outlook* (*Booker T. Washington,* 293), a further indication of Park's role in the text's authorship.
57. Matthew Alexander Henson, *A Negro Explorer at the North Pole* (1912; Montpelier, Vt.: Invisible Cities Press, 2001); review of *A Negro Explorer at the North Pole, The Outlook,* March 9, 1912, 558.
58. Booker T. Washington, introduction to Henson, *A Negro Explorer at the North Pole,* xxxii; Robert E. Peary, foreword, ibid., xxvii; Washington, introduction, ibid., xxxiii.
59. "Some Notable Educational Enterprises: Tuskegee Institute," *The Outlook,* March 30, 1912, 708–9.
60. Washington, *The Man Farthest Down,* 15. Winifred Raushenbush notes that while Park was willing to collaborate anonymously on two earlier books, *The Story of the Negro* (1909) and *My Larger Education* (1911), he asked for equal billing as co-author of *The Man Farthest Down.* (*Robert E. Park: Biography of a Sociologist* [Durham: Duke University Press, 1979], 56). Washington did not agree to sign the book jointly with Park, but in the first chapter he does explain his dependence on Park's data and observations, and the title page indicates that the book was written "with the collaboration of Robert E. Park." Despite Park's important contributions to the book, Drake suggests that because "Washington had dictated the backbone of the work in the first person, it would have been inappropriate to speak of the men as co-authors" (introduction, xxiii). The choice of narrative voice does not diminish Park's role in co-authoring this as well as other

of Washington's published works, however, for as Harlan observes, Park "researched, drafted, or revised most of Washington's writings for publication between 1905 and 1912" (*Booker T. Washington,* 291).

61. Washington, *The Man Farthest Down,* 15, 17, 269–70.
62. Ibid., 205–7, 249–50, 279–80, 287, 290–91, 293–95.
63. Ibid., 122–23, 342, 343, 358–59.
64. Ibid., 54–55, 84–85, 95, 109.
65. Farah Jasmine Griffin, *"Who Set You Flowin'?": The African-American Migration Narrative* (New York: Oxford University Press, 1995), 9.
66. Frances Bartkowski, *Travelers, Immigrants, Inmates: Essays in Estrangement* (Minneapolis: University of Minnesota Press, 1995), 101.
67. Washington, *The Man Farthest Down,* 389–90.
68. Raushenbush, *Robert E. Park,* 56.
69. Washington's text continues to serve such a purpose. Joseph A. D'Agostino quotes Harry Alford of the National Black Chamber of Commerce, who stated in 2004 that *The Man Farthest Down* is "even more relevant" than *Up from Slavery* for African American readers today, as it "shows that the descendants of slaves were not farthest down" ("Conservative Spotlight: National Black Chamber of Commerce," *Human Events: Powerful Conservative Voices,* August 5, 2004, www.humanevents.com).

3. "TO RETURN AND TELL THE TALE OF THE DOING"

1. Matthew Henson, *A Negro Explorer at the North Pole* (1912; Montpelier, Vt.: Invisible Cities Press, 2001), 98–99, 101.
2. Tim Youngs "Pushing against the Black/White Limits of Maps: African American Writings of Travel," *English Studies in Africa* 53, no. 2 (2010): 71.
3. S. Allen Counter, *North Pole Legacy: Black, White, and Eskimo* (Montpelier, Vt.: Invisible Cities Press, 2001), 73.
4. Booker T. Washington, introduction to Henson, *A Negro Explorer at the North Pole,* xxxii–iv.
5. James Olney, "'I Was Born': Slave Narratives, Their Status as Autobiography and as Literature," *Callaloo* 20 (Winter 1984): 50, 52. Another way that slave narratives are legitimized, according to Olney, is through appendices of documentary materials, including "bills of sale, details of purchase from slavery, [or] newspaper items" (51). Although Henson did not include such items in his narrative, Peary included quite a few in the appendices of his North Pole narrative to prove the validity of the discovery and to establish his authority. A website maintained by the Matthew Henson Society (www.matthewhenson.com) amasses documentary materials about Henson and his descendants, but it does not provide detailed bibliographic information for sources.
6. Henson, *A Negro Explorer at the North Pole,* 2.
7. Ibid., 120, 53, 89, 84, 125, 28, 47.
8. Olney, "I Was Born," 50; Frederick Douglass, *Narrative of the Life of Frederick Douglass, An American Slave. Written by Himself* (1845), in *The Classic Slave Narratives,* ed. Henry Louis Gates Jr. (New York: Penguin, 1987), 281.
9. Olaudah Equiano, *The Interesting Narrative of the Life of Olaudah Equiano: Written by Himself* (1791; Boston: Bedford Books, 1995), 149, 30.
10. Henson, *A Negro Explorer at the North Pole,* 84.

11. Anthony S. Foy, "Matthew Henson and the Antinomies of Racial Uplift," *a/b: Auto/Biography Studies* 27, no. 1 (2012): 25. Foy concludes that "the full success of Peary's expedition depends on the racialization of servile labor that casts Henson as a mere shadow in the heart of whiteness. The tragic crisis at the core of this memoir calls into question the elevating potential of meritocracy, exposing the racial fissures that disrupt the Washingtonian discourse of synecdochic recognition through work" (39).
12. Molefi Kete Asante has suggested that the more Henson traveled with Peary, the more "Peary began to see him as his trusted fellow explorer" (*The African American People: A Global History* [New York: Routledge, 2012], 131), though this is not necessarily borne out by Henson's or Peary's account of the North Pole expedition.
13. Robert E. Peary, *The North Pole: Its Discovery in 1909 under the Auspices of the Peary Arctic Club* (New York: Frederick A. Stokes, 1910), 326, 20, 109, 172, 272.
14. Lowell Thomas, "First at the Pole," *This Week* magazine, *New York Herald Tribune*, April 2, 1939, transcription at www.matthewhenson.com, 5, 7.
15. Peary, *The North Pole*, 272, 273.
16. Theodore Roosevelt, introduction to Peary, *The North Pole*, vii–viii.
17. Henson, *A Negro Explorer at the North Pole*, 101; Matthew Henson, "Matt Henson Tells the Real Story of Peary's Trip to Pole," in *A Negro Explorer at the North Pole*, 149.
18. Roosevelt, introduction, viii; Gilbert H. Grosvenor, foreword to Peary, *The North Pole*, xxxii. Roosevelt in his introduction emphasizes his own status as an explorer. He notes that he receives word of Peary's discovery from "a native runner" while "camped on the northern foothills of Mt. Kenia, directly under the equator" (vi), and he signs the introduction from the midst of his exploration work in "The White Nile, March 12, 1910" (viii).
19. Richard C. Davis, "From Conquest to Cognition: 20th Century Exploration Narratives," *Arctic* 34, no. 1 (March 1981): 85–86.
20. Peary, *The North Pole*, 297.
21. Thomas, "First at the Pole," 3.
22. Davis, "From Conquest to Cognition," 86.
23. Roy Bridges, "Exploration and Travel Outside Europe (1720–1914)," in *The Cambridge Companion to Travel Writing*, ed. Peter Hulme and Tim Youngs (Cambridge: Cambridge University Press, 2002), 54.
24. Cook claimed to have discovered the pole a full year before Peary and Henson, and the issue is still debated. Henson states near the end of *Negro Explorer* that all the "debts of gratitude" he owes Cook for being invited to live with his parents while suffering from snow blindness "have been liquidated" by his silence about the controversy (128).
25. Roosevelt, introduction, vii.
26. Peary, *The North Pole*, 350.
27. Henson, "Matt Henson Tells the Real Story," 147, 148.
28. Review of *A Negro Explorer at the North Pole*, *New York Times*, March 17, 1912; "A Negro at the Pole," *The Nation*, April 11, 1912, 369.
29. Henson, *A Negro Explorer at the North Pole*, 101.
30. Peary, *The North Pole*, 241.
31. Henson, *A Negro Explorer at the North Pole*, 55, 67, 29, 2.
32. Ibid., 21, 16, 53, 60, 61.
33. Equiano, *The Interesting Narrative*, 125.
34. Peary, *The North Pole*, 272.

35. Henson, *A Negro Explorer at the North Pole,* 12, 15.
36. Henson, "Matt Henson Tells the Real Story," 152.
37. Henson, *A Negro Explorer at the North Pole,* 26, 27.
38. Ibid., 31, 37.
39. Ibid., 63, 65, 71.
40. Stephanie Leigh Batiste, *Darkening Mirrors: Imperial Representation in Depression-Era African American Performance* (Durham: Duke University Press, 2011), xiii, 4.
41. Henson, *A Negro Explorer at the North Pole,* 4. Foy describes Henson's interactions with the Eskimo members of the party as a process of "enact[ing] his own uplift by civilizing . . . the Native" ("Matthew Henson and the Antinomies of Racial Uplift," 31).
42. Nicolás Wey Gómez, *Tropics of Empire: Why Columbus Sailed South to the Indies* (Cambridge: MIT Press, 2008).
43. "Negroes Banquet Matthew Henson," *New York Age,* October 21, 1909, 2.
44. Foy, "Matthew Henson and the Antinomies of Racial Uplift," 22.
45. Henson, *A Negro Explorer at the North Pole,* 32.
46. Popular stereotypes about the dirt and disease of the Other appeared in early twentieth-century discourse and print culture. For example, in 1913, Richard Barry linked European immigrants with New York City's sanitation and health problems ("A War Worth Waging: The Successful Fight to Improve the Health of New York City," *Century Magazine,* May 1913, 32). In 1916, Burton J. Hendrick noted how U.S. concepts of hygiene and public health improved conditions in the Philippines, despite stereotypes connecting disease and the Orient ("An American Who Made Health Contagious," *Harper's Magazine,* April 1916, 717), but Hendrick sustains the stereotypes supporting this connection by characterizing Filipinos as superstitious, barbaric, and exotic. (See also Warwick Anderson, *Colonial Pathologies: American Tropical Medicine, Race, and Hygiene in the Philippines* [Durham: Duke University Press, 2006], on how these connections facilitated American colonialism in the Philippines.) The fear that immigrant groups would spread disease among the native U.S. population (Alan M. Kraut, *Silent Travelers: Germs, Genes, and the Immigrant Menace* [New York: Basic Books, 1994], 3–4) contributed to the notion of the Irish as Other, as evident in the reaction to the 1918 flu epidemic in Norwood, Massachusetts, which newspapers blamed on the "unsanitary living conditions, deficient personal hygiene, and lack of assimilation" of Irish immigrants (Patricia J. Fanning, "Epidemics, Influenza, and the Irish: Norwood, Massachusetts, in 1918," in *New Perspectives on the Irish Diaspora,* ed. Charles Fanning [Carbondale: Southern Illinois University Press, 2000], 226). Such stereotypes had existed since the early nineteenth century; for example, in the 1830s, Irish immigrants were considered the cause of the cholera epidemic (Alan M. Kraut "Plagues and Prejudice: Nativism's Construction of Disease in Nineteenth- and Twentieth-Century New York City," in *Hives of Sickness: Public Health and Epidemics in New York City,* ed. David Rosner [New Brunswick: Rutgers University Press, 1995], 67).
47. Henson, *A Negro Explorer at the North Pole,* 35.
48. Ann Fienup-Riordan, *Eskimo Essays: Yup'ik Lives and How We See Them* (New Brunswick: Rutgers University Press, 1990), 14, 15.
49. Ibid., 15; Robert E. Peary, *Northward Over the "Great Ice": A Narrative of Life and Work along the Shores and upon the Interior Ice-Cap of Northern Greenland in the Years 1886 and 1891–1897,* vol. 1 (London: Methuen, 1898), 483.
50. Fienup-Riordan, *Eskimo Essays,* 15.

51. Henson, *A Negro Explorer at the North Pole,* 36, 47.
52. Ibid., 66.
53. Ibid., 90.
54. Ibid., 93, 95; Henson, "Matt Henson Tells the Real Story," 148.
55. Thomas, "First at the Pole," 2.
56. Matthew Henson, "The Negro at the North Pole: The Story of the Last Dash, Told by Commander Peary's Only American Companion at the Top of the Earth," *The World's Work: A History of Our Time* 19 (April 1910): 12837.
57. Henson, *A Negro Explorer at the North Pole,* 98–99.
58. Langston Hughes, "The Negro Speaks of Rivers," *The Crisis,* June 1921, 71.
59. Henson, *A Negro Explorer at the North Pole,* 99, 102.
60. Henson, "Matt Henson Tells the Real Story," 147.
61. Henson also includes the photo of himself and the Eskimos in his narrative, but he uses as a frontispiece a photo of himself in his Arctic clothing that is a close-up of his face. Peary's self-portrait frontispiece is a full-length shot of him in "Actual North Pole Costume," on snowshoes and holding a spear. He looks straight at the camera with a serious expression on his face. Peary's portrait suggests he is a man of action and conquest while Henson's portrait is much more personal and casts him as a more approachable individual. Like Peary, Henson looks straight at the camera, but the close-up focuses the viewer's attention on his welcoming and even congenial facial expression. Projecting a somewhat more conventionally authoritative persona in his 1909 *World's Work* article on the discovery, Henson includes a full-length photograph of himself—similar to Peary's—with the caption "The Negro Who Reached the Pole" and Peary's statement "Probably a better dog-driver than any other man living, except some of the best Eskimo hunters themselves" (12826).
62. "Borup Tells How Grit Won the Pole," *New York Times,* September 20, 1909, 3.
63. Counter, *North Pole Legacy,* 75. Appendix 3 in Peary's North Pole narrative includes a lengthy list of the medals, honorary doctorates, memberships, and other honors that Peary received for his exploration work.
64. Henson, *A Negro Explorer at the North Pole,* 102, 103.
65. Ibid., 94–97.
66. Henson, "Matt Henson Tells the Real Story," 147–48.
67. Henson, *A Negro Explorer at the North Pole,* 98.
68. Matthew Henson, "1910 Testimony from Matt Henson," transcribed from *Hampton's Magazine* (1910), www.matthewhenson.com; Thomas, "First at the Pole," 4.
69. The passage of time appears to have further softened Henson's characterization of his relationship with Peary. In a 1932 *New York Times* interview, Henson describes a more congenial and collaborative process of discovery, noting, "Peary took the sights while I made notes in his book." After checking the observations, Peary exclaims, "My boy, do you think we have reached the Pole?" Henson adds: "I said I believed we had. He assured me our observations were accurate to gauge our position within a mile" ("Looking Back across the Ice," *New York Times,* April 17, 1932).
70. Henson, *A Negro Explorer at the North Pole,* 99.
71. Francis Smith Foster, *Witnessing Slavery: The Development of Ante-Bellum Slave Narratives,* 2nd ed. (Madison: University of Wisconsin Press, 1979), 70.
72. Henson, *A Negro Explorer at the North Pole,* 102.
73. Davis, "From Conquest to Cognition," 86.

74. Henson, "Matt Henson Tells the True Story," 146–47, 149–51.
75. Frances Smith Foster has helpfully situated the slave narrative in the context of the sentimental novel tradition. Considering sales and audience appeal in the nineteenth century, Foster places the slave narrative somewhere between the best-selling sentimental novels and works by Thoreau, Melville, and Hawthorne that did not enjoy mass popularity (*Witnessing Slavery,* 22–23).
76. Christine Levecq, *Slavery and Sentiment: The Politics of Feeling in Black Atlantic Antislavery Writing, 1770–1850* (Lebanon: University of New Hampshire Press, 2008), ix.
77. Hazel Carby, *Reconstructing Womanhood: The Emergence of the Afro-American Woman Novelist* (New York: Oxford University Press, 1987); Karen Sánchez-Eppler, *Touching Liberty: Abolition, Feminism, and the Politics of the Body* (Berkeley: University of California Press, 1993); Cindy Weinstein, "The Slave Narrative and Sentimental Literature," in *The Cambridge Companion to the African American Slave Narrative,* ed. Audrey A. Fisch (Cambridge: Cambridge University Press, 2007), 117, 131.
78. For a discussion of neo–slave narratives and critical reactions to the form, see Valerie Smith, "Neo–Slave Narratives," in *The Cambridge Companion to the African American Slave Narrative,* 168–85.
79. Keith Byerman, *Remembering the Past in Contemporary African American Fiction* (Chapel Hill: University of North Carolina Press, 2005), 33, 35.
80. A. Timothy Spaulding, *Re-forming the Past: History, the Fantastic, and the Postmodern Slave Narrative* (Columbus: Ohio State University Press, 2005), 63.
81. See Gary Totten, "Re-authoring the Nineteenth Century: Morrison's *Beloved* and Stowe's *Uncle Tom's Cabin,*" in *Inhabited by Stories: Critical Essays on Tales Retold,* ed. Nancy Barta-Smith and Danette DiMarco (Cambridge: Cambridge Scholar's Press, 2012), 214–31.
82. Henson, "Matt Henson Tells the Real Story," 147.
83. Henson, *A Negro Explorer at the North Pole,* 111.
84. The rift is tempered somewhat by Henson's claim in a 1939 article in *Ken* magazine that "Mister Peary was a noble man, and it was a privilege to serve him. He was always my friend" (quoted in Carl John Bostelmann, "Discovery of the Unsung Hero of Polar Discovery," *Ken,* June 15, 1939, 14).
85. Paul Smethurst, introduction to *Travel Writing, Form, and Empire: The Poetics and Politics of Mobility,* ed. Julia Kuehn and Paul Smethurst (New York: Routledge, 2009), 2.
86. Davis, "From Conquest to Cognition," 87.

4. CULTURAL WORK, DISORDERLY MOBILITY, AND THE MUNDANE REALITIES OF TRAVEL

1. Carolyn Wedin Sylvander notes that the position of Fauset's father, Redmon Fauset, as an A.M.E. minister would have put her family "a step up the cultural ladder," but the family did not enjoy the economic position that would allow us to call them "middle class or prosperous or socially established" (*Jessie Redmon Fauset, Black American Writer* [Troy, N.Y.: Whitston Publishing Co., 1981], 24, 26). Similarly, Cheryl A. Wall observes that "the legacy Redmon Fauset bequeathed to his children inhered in the values he imparted; the family had little money. . . . But his calling ensured respectability, if not prosperity," values revealed in Fauset's February 1922 *Crisis* essay "Sunday Afternoon" (162–64) (*Women of the Harlem Renaissance* [Bloomington: Indiana University Press,

1995], 39). Abby Arthur Johnson suggests that "the atmosphere of the parsonage remained with her" ("Literary Midwife: Jessie Redmon Fauset and the Harlem Renaissance," *Phylon* 39, no. 2 [1978]: 150), and Fauset herself wrote in an autobiographical note in Countee Cullen's edited volume *Caroling Dusk,* "I am fond of dancing, and adore cards and the theatre probably because I am a minister's daughter" (*Caroling Dusk: An Anthology of Verse by Negro Poets* [New York: Harper and Bros., 1927], 65). Fauset's penchant for Christian metaphor is evident in her January 1926 *Crisis* article about her experiences abroad, "The Eucalyptus Tree," provocatively subtitled "A Reverie of Rome, the Catacombs, Christianity and the Moving Beauty of Italy" (116–17). Her descriptions are graphic and gothic as she recounts the eerie experience of touring the catacombs; considering what it would be like to be lost in the subterranean caverns, she thinks that "sudden death would be sweeter." Coming out of the catacombs into the light, she sees a eucalyptus tree, which she describes in great detail, noting the sound that the wind makes in its foliage, "like the running of a rivulet composed of all those tears which Christians had shed in those terrible days of doom and death" symbolized by the catacombs below. "The roots of the eucalyptus tree are plunged deep in that cemetery but its branches bear a beneficent sap within their veins. Baffled, beaten, its beginnings in catacombs of doubt, misinterpretation, tears, Christianity yet rises, rises with healing in its wings" (117). Fauset's elaborate metaphor is instructive, as it emphasizes a conservative Christianity underpinning her impressions.

2. Jessie Redmon Fauset, "Some Notes on Color," *The World Tomorrow,* March 1922, 77.
3. Michel Fabre, *From Harlem to Paris: Black American Writers in France, 1840–1980* (Urbana: University of Illinois Press, 1991), 116.
4. Jessie Redmon Fauset to Joel Spingarn, January 25, 1922, Joel E. Spingarn Papers, New York Public Library; Fabre, *From Harlem to Paris,* 116.
5. Cheryl A. Wall, *Women of the Harlem Renaissance,* 48.
6. Farah J. Griffin and Cheryl J. Fish, eds., *A Stranger in the Village: Two Centuries of African-American Travel Writing* (Boston: Beacon Press, 1998), 180.
7. Deborah McDowell, "Introduction: Regulating Midwives," in *Plum Bun: A Novel without a Moral* (1929) by Jessie Redmon Fauset (Boston: Beacon Press, 1990), xii.
8. Sterling Brown, *Negro Poetry and Drama* and *The Negro in American Fiction* (1937; New York: Atheneum, 1969), 142; Robert Bone, *The Negro Novel in America* (New Haven: Yale University Press, 1965), 101.
9. W. E. B. Du Bois and Alain Locke, "The Younger Literary Movement," *The Crisis,* February 1924, 161, 162, 163.
10. Advertisement for *There Is Confusion* by Jessie Redmon Fauset, *The Crisis,* April 1924, 284.
11. Alain Locke, "The Saving Grace of Realism: Retrospective Review of the Negro Literature of 1933," *Opportunity,* January 1934, 9.
12. Kathleen Pfeiffer, "The Limits of Identity in Jessie Fauset's *Plum Bun,*" *Legacy: A Journal of American Women Writers* 18, no.1 (2001): 80.
13. Langston Hughes, *The Big Sea* (New York: Alfred A. Knopf, 1940), 218.
14. Jessie Redmon Fauset to Langston Hughes, May 28, 1923; June 24, 1924; January 6, 1925; October 14, 1925; and October 23, 1925, Yale Collection of American Literature, Beinecke Rare Book and Manuscript Library.
15. Jessie Redmon Fauset, "New Literature on the Negro," *The Crisis,* June 1920, 78–83; Johnson, "Literary Midwife," 146.

16. Claude McKay, *A Long Way from Home* (New York: Lee Furman, 1937), 112.
17. Jessie Redmon Fauset, "The Negro in Art: How Shall He Be Portrayed? A Symposium," *The Crisis,* June 1926, 71–72.
18. Jessie Redmon Fauset to Langston Hughes, June 24, 1924, and April 14, 1922, Yale Collection of American Literature, Beinecke Rare Book and Manuscript Library.
19. Gerald Sykes, "Amber-Tinted Elegance," *The Nation,* July 27, 1932, 88.
20. Leroi Jones, "The Myth of A 'Negro Literature,'" in *On Being Black: Writings by Afro-Americans from Frederick Douglass to the Present,* ed. Charles T. Davis and Daniel Walden (Greenwich, Conn.: Fawcett, 1970), 294.
21. Evelyn Brooks Higginbotham, *Righteous Discontent: The Women's Movement in the Black Baptist Church, 1880–1920* (Cambridge: Harvard University Press, 1993), 186, 187, 16–17.
22. Sylvander, *Jessie Redmon Fauset,* 5.
23. Higginbotham, *Righteous Discontent,* 186.
24. "The Third Pan-African Congress." *The Crisis,* January 1924, 120, 121.
25. For the full text of the bill, see "Bill H. R. 1 The Dyer Anti-Lynching Bill," *The Crisis,* February 1924, 164–65.
26. "Financing the Fight against Lynching," *The Crisis,* January 1924, 124.
27. As another example, Du Bois prints in his *Crisis* "Opinion" column of June 1924 a response from E. Franklin Frazier, whose March article, "The Negro and Non-Resistance," drew criticism from readers. In his June 1924 response, Frazier does not specifically condone violence, but he does suggest that oppressed peoples gain more justice when they show a "disposition . . . to retaliate" (58).
28. Jessie Redmon Fauset, "Rencontre," *The Crisis,* January 1924, 122.
29. Wall, *Women of the Harlem Renaissance,* 58.
30. Jessie Redmon Fauset to Langston Hughes, June 24, 1924, Yale Collection of American Literature, Beinecke Rare Book and Manuscript Library.
31. Wall, *Women of the Harlem Renaissance,* 57, 66.
32. Deborah E. McDowell, "The Neglected Dimension of Jessie Fauset," in *Conjuring: Black Women, Fiction, and Tradition,* ed. Marjorie Pryse and Hortense J. Spillers (Bloomington: Indiana University Press, 1985), 87.
33. Sylvander, *Jessie Redmon Fauset,* 43.
34. Charles S. Johnson, "The Rise of the Negro Magazine," *Journal of Negro History* 13, no. 1 (January 1928): 9; Sylvander, *Jessie Redmon Fauset,* 43.
35. "The Horizon," *The Crisis,* January 1924, 129–35.
36. Teresa Zackodnik, "Recirculation and Feminist Black Internationalism in Jessie Fauset's 'The Looking Glass' and Amy Jacques Garvey's 'Our Women and What They Think,'" *Modernism/modernity* 19, no. 3 (September 2012): 440.
37. "The Looking Glass," *The Crisis,* January 1924, 127.
38. Zackodnik, "Recirculation and Feminist Black Internationalism," 440.
39. Stephen Greenblatt, "Culture," in *Critical Terms for Literary Study,* 2nd ed., ed. Frank Lentricchia and Thomas McLaughlin (Chicago: University of Chicago Press, 1995), 228–29.
40. W. E. B. Du Bois, "Opinion of W. E. B. Du Bois," *The Crisis,* September 1924, 202, 203.
41. Sylvander, *Jessie Redmon Fauset,* 10.
42. Sterling Brown, "The Negro Author and His Publisher," *Negro Quarterly,* 1 (Spring 1942): 14, 15.

43. Sylvander, *Jessie Redmon Fauset,* 10, 13–14.
44. Clara G. Stillman, "A Tourist in Florida," *The Crisis,* January 1924, 107.
45. Ibid.
46. Ibid., 108.
47. Stillman, "A Tourist in Florida," *The Crisis,* February 1924, 173.
48. Ibid., 173–74.
49. Claude McKay, "Soviet Russia and the Negro," *The Crisis,* January 1924, 115, 116.
50. Countee Cullen, "Yet Do I Marvel," in *Color* (New York: Harper and Bros, 1925), 3.
51. McKay, "Soviet Russia and the Negro," 116, 117.
52. W. E. B. Du Bois, "Opinion of W. E. B. Du Bois," *The Crisis,* April 1924, 247, 250.
53. W. E. B. Du Bois, "Opinion of W. E. B. Du Bois," *The Crisis,* March 1924, 202.
54. Du Bois, "Opinion," April 1924, 250.
55. W. E. B. Du Bois, "Little Portraits of Africa," *The Crisis,* April 1924, 273, 274.
56. W. E. B. Du Bois, "Opinion of W. E. B. Du Bois," *The Crisis,* June 1924, 58.
57. Fauset's travel writing also emphasizes her international experience, and, with the essays of Du Bois, McKay, and others, highlights the international scope of the magazine itself. As one example, Fauset's translations of excerpts from French scholars' work on Africa demonstrates this international reach. In "La Question des Noirs Aux Etats-Unis" in the June 1924 issue, Fauset translates selections from Frank L. Schoell's 1923 book of the same name, arguing that the text "throws a significant light on the increasing realization on the part of Europe and particularly on the part of France that the American Negro is looming large in ordering the affairs of the black world." Not surprisingly, the selections that Fauset translates cast Du Bois in a positive light; Schoell notes how *The Souls of Black Folk* (1903) and *The Crisis* indicate Du Bois's awareness of the way "his own small black American world" fits into "the *ensemble* of the great, the titanic black world of Africa." These texts are contrasted with *The Future of the American Negro* (1899) by Booker T. Washington, which Schoell castigates for its provincialism and lack of interest in Africa ("La Question des Noirs," 83). Schoell also notes Du Bois's influence on Marcus Garvey and the pan-African movement and discusses the Pan-African Congresses, again remarking on Du Bois's major role in these gatherings. See also Zackodnik, "Recirculation and Feminist Black Internationalism," for a discussion of the overlooked importance of Fauset's internationalism.
58. Paul Smethurst, introduction to *Travel Writing, Form, and Empire: The Poetics and Politics of Mobility,* ed. Julia Kuehn and Paul Smethurst (New York: Routledge, 2009), 7, 2; Edward W. Said, *Orientalism* (New York: Pantheon, 1978).
59. Sylvander, *Jessie Redmon Fauset,* 69.
60. Langston Hughes, "The Fascination of Cities," *The Crisis,* January 1926, 138–40.
61. Jessie Redmon Fauset, "Yarrow Revisited," *The Crisis,* January 1925, 109.
62. "The Great American Specialty: Lynchings of 1923," *The Crisis,* February 1924, 168.
63. Fauset, "Some Notes on Color," 77.
64. "110 Delegates to the Pan-African Congress by Countries," *The Crisis,* December 1921, 68.
65. Jessie Redmon Fauset, "What Europe Thought of the Pan-African Congress," *The Crisis,* December 1921, 66.
66. Jessie Redmon Fauset, "Impressions of the Second Pan-African Congress," *The Crisis,* November 1921, 14.
67. Wall, *Women of the Harlem Renaissance,* 49; Fauset, "Impressions," 15. As Eve E. Dun-

bar notes, Zora Neale Hurston too draws overly broad parallels between racial politics in the United States and conditions in the Caribbean (*Black Regions of the Imagination: African American Writers between the Nation and the World* [Philadelphia: Temple University Press, 2013], 50).

68. Jessie Redmon Fauset, "Nostalgia," *The Crisis,* August 1921, 157, 158; Fauset, "Yarrow Revisited," 109.
69. Fauset, "Yarrow Revisited," 107.
70. Ibid., 107, 108.
71. Ibid., 108.
72. Ibid., 108, 109.
73. Ibid., 109; Fauset, "Impressions," 12.
74. Fauset, "Yarrow Revisited," 109.
75. Jessie Redmon Fauset to Langston Hughes, January 6, 1925, Yale Collection of American Literature, Beinecke Rare Book and Manuscript Library; *Paris Herald Tribune* interview quoted in Shari Benstock, *Women of the Left Bank: Paris, 1900–1940* (Austin: University of Texas Press, 1986), 13.
76. Quoted in Wall, *Women of the Harlem Renaissance,* 72.
77. James Weldon Johnson, *Along This Way: The Autobiography of James Weldon Johnson* (New York: Viking, 1933), 209.
78. W. E. B. Du Bois, *Darkwater: Voices from Within the Veil* (New York: Harcourt, Brace and Howe, 1920), 16.
79. Jessie Redmon Fauset, "This Way to the Flea Market," *The Crisis,* February 1925, 161, 162.
80. Ibid., 162, 163.
81. Ibid., 163.
82. Jessie Redmon Fauset, "The Enigma of the Sorbonne," *The Crisis,* March 1925, 216.
83. Sylvander, *Jessie Redmon Fauset,* 2. Fauset was long thought to be the first black women in the United States to be admitted to Phi Beta Kappa, but more recent research has turned up an earlier inductee, Mary Anderson (at Middlebury College in 1899); see Caldwell Titcomb, "New Discovery of an Earlier Black Female Member of Phi Beta Kappa," *Journal of Blacks in Higher Education* 45 (Autumn 2004): 95–97. According to Sylvander, a note on Fauset's alumni address card written by George Lincoln Burr, a longtime professor of history at Cornell, indicates that she was the only "colored student" elected to Phi Beta Kappa at the school until 1921 (30).
84. Fauset, "The Enigma of the Sorbonne," 219.
85. Jessie Redmon Fauset, "Dark Algiers the White: Part I," *The Crisis,* April 1925, 255–56.
86. Wall, *Women of the Harlem Renaissance,* 34.
87. Fauset, "Dark Algiers the White: Part I," 256.
88. Ibid., 256.
89. Stillman, "A Tourist in Florida," 107.
90. Fauset, "Dark Algiers the White: Part I," 256.
91. Ibid., 257, 258.
92. Ibid., 258.
93. Wall, *Women of the Harlem Renaissance,* 38.
94. Fauset, "Dark Algiers, The White: Part I," 258. This reference to phrenology invokes the emphasis on racial characteristics and fitness germane to the eugenics issue, which was debated in *The Crisis.* Albert Sidney Beckham, in his article "Applied Eugenics,"

argued, among other things, that "eugenics can only help the Negro in respect to the degree in which he controls his mating. . . . It is fundamental to note that persons of like undesirable traits should not mate. . . . The future problems of the Negro will be the elimination of the unfit and the perpetuation of the fit" (*The Crisis,* August 1924, 178). E. Franklin Frazier published a rejoinder in December 1925 about "the limitations of eugenic control in the race problem," noting that "the Negro problem is essentially a problem of social adjustment" and psychology ("Eugenics and the Race Problem," *The Crisis,* December 1925, 91). In his address to the NAACP, "Science, Pseudo-Science and the Race Question," reprinted in the October 1925 *Crisis,* Herbert Adolphus Miller claimed that scientific thought related to the race question is a pseudo-science, because "a race is an artificial division of the human race for the purposes of classification" (291).

95. Fauset, "Dark Algiers the White: Part I," 258.
96. Jessie Redmon Fauset, "Dark Algiers the White: Part II," *The Crisis,* May 1925, 16.
97. Ibid., 16, 17.
98. Wall, *Women of the Harlem Renaissance,* 34.
99. Fauset, "Dark Algiers the White: Part II," 17.
100. Wall, *Women of the Harlem Renaissance,* 34.
101. Fauset, "Dark Algiers the White: Part II," 17, 18.
102. Wall, *Women of the Harlem Renaissance,* 35.
103. Smethurst, introduction, 7, 8.
104. Fauset, "Dark Algiers the White: Part II," 19.
105. Ibid., 20.
106. Smethurst, introduction, 10, 12.
107. Jessie Redmon Fauset, "Episodes in Tangier," *The Metropolitan: A Monthly Review,* January 1935, 8.
108. Ibid., 8, 9.
109. Ibid., 9.

5. BODIES OF KNOWLEDGE

1. Marguerite Helmers and Tilar J. Mazzeo, "Introduction: Travel and the Body," *Journal of Narrative Theory* 35, no. 3 (2005): 267.
2. Lila M. Harper, *Solitary Travelers: Nineteenth-Century Women's Travel Narratives and the Scientific Vocation* (Madison, N.J.: Fairleigh Dickinson University Press, 2001); Sara Mills, *Discourses of Difference: An Analysis of Women's Travel Writing and Colonialism* (New York: Routledge, 1991).
3. Zora Neale Hurston, *Dust Tracks on a Road: An Autobiography,* 2nd ed., ed. Robert Hemenway (1942; Urbana: University of Illinois Press, 1984), 212.
4. Zora Neale Hurston, *Tell My Horse* (Philadelphia: J. B. Lippincott, 1938), 156, 206, 415, 475. Hurston uses the term "voodoo" in her text, as I do here. For a discussion of variants, see Alasdair Pettinger, "From Vaudoux to Voodoo," *Forum for Modern Language Studies* 40, no. 4 (2004): 415–25.
5. *Zora Neale Hurston: A Life in Letters,* ed. Carla Kaplan (New York: Doubleday, 2002), 386, 381.
6. Hortense J. Spillers, "Mama's Baby, Papa's Maybe: An American Grammar Book," *Diacritics* 17, no. 2 (1987): 72.

7. For scholars who emphasize the gendered experience of the Middle Passage, see Deborah Gray White, *Ar'n't I a Woman: Female Slaves in the Plantation South* (New York: Norton, 1985); and Robyn Wiegman, *American Anatomies: Theorizing Race and Gender* (Durham: Duke University Press, 1995), 65–67. Wiegman in particular examines Spillers's contention in "Mama's Baby, Papa's Maybe" that the Middle Passage experience is ungendered.
8. Ronald E. Martin, *The Languages of Difference: American Writers and Anthropologists Reconfigure the Primitive, 1878–1940* (Newark: University of Delaware Press, 2005), 234–63; Hemenway, introduction to Hurston, *Dust Tracks on a Road,* xviii; Robert E. Hemenway, *Zora Neale Hurston: A Literary Biography* (Urbana: University of Illinois Press, 1977), 213.
9. Quoted in Valerie Boyd, *Wrapped in Rainbows: The Life of Zora Neale Hurston* (New York: Scribner, 2003), 269–70.
10. Richard Wright, "Between Laughter and Tears," *New Masses,* October 5, 1937, 25.
11. Ralph Ellison, "Recent Negro Fiction," *New Masses,* August 5, 1941, 24.
12. Otis Ferguson, "You Can't Hear Their Voices," *New Republic,* October 13, 1937, 276.
13. Alain Locke, "Jingo, Counter-Jingo and Us," *Opportunity,* January 1938, 10.
14. Zora Neale Hurston, "Art and Such" (1938), in *Zora Neale Hurston: Folklore, Memoirs, and Other Writings,* ed. Cheryl A Wall (New York: Library of America, 1995), 906–8. Contemporary critics such as Valerie Boyd also find psychological and emotional depth and social importance in Hurston's fiction. Of *Their Eyes,* Boyd claims the novel succeeds as both a love story and a protest novel (*Wrapped in Rainbows,* 304–5).
15. George Stevens, "Negroes by Themselves," *Saturday Review of Literature,* September 18, 1937, 3.
16. Lucy Tompkins, "In the Florida Glades," *New York Times Book Review,* September 26, 1937, 29.
17. Sheila Hibben, "Vibrant Book Full of Nature and Salt," *New York Herald Tribune Weekly Book Review,* September 26, 1937, 2.
18. *Zora Neale Hurston: A Life in Letters,* 392 (emphasis added), 400, 384, 385, 386n1, 387. Hurston refers to Herskovits's advice that she leave Jamaica for the Bahamas in an undated letter to Henry Moe, probably written in April or May 1936 (376).
19. Ibid., 372.
20. Deborah G. Plant, *Zora Neale Hurston: A Biography of the Spirit* (Westport, Conn.: Praeger, 2007), 43–47; Kevin Meehan, "Decolonizing Ethnography: Zora Neale Hurston in the Caribbean," in *Women at Sea: Travel Writing and the Margins of Caribbean Discourse,* ed. Lizabeth Paravisini-Gebert and Ivette Romero-Cesareo (New York: Palgrave, 2001), 245–46; Tiffany Ruby Patterson, *Zora Neale Hurston and a History of Southern Life* (Philadelphia: Temple University Press, 2005), 29, 23; Alice Walker, "Zora Neale Hurston: A Cautionary Tale and a Partisan View," in *In Search of Our Mothers' Gardens* (San Diego: Harcourt, Brace, Jovanovich, 1983), 87. Dorothea Fischer-Hornung notes that a new context for Hurston's work has been created by disciplinary shifts in anthropology since the 1980s, including "the increasing emphasis on the fundamentally narrative nature of anthropological discourse as well as research on the gendered and racialized proclivities of the academy" ("'Keep Alive the Powers of Africa': Katherine Dunham, Zora Neale Hurston, Maya Deren, and the Circum-Caribbean Culture of Vodoun," *Atlantic Studies* 5, no. 3 [December 2008]: 350). See also James Clifford, *The Predicament of Culture: Twentieth-Century Ethnography, Literature, and Art*

(Cambridge: Harvard University Press, 1988); George E. Marcus, *Ethnography through Thick and Thin* (Princeton: Princeton University Press, 1998); and Nancy J. Parezo, ed., *Hidden Scholars: Women Anthropologists and the Native American Southwest* (Albuquerque: University of New Mexico Press, 1993).

21. Kevin Meehan, Dorothea Fischer-Hornung, and Frances Bartkowski discuss *Tell My Horse* as a travel text but not explicitly in terms of Hurston's mobility. Meehan focuses on Hurston's strategy to "decolonize ethnography" through her portrayal of native informants and "the gendered and gendering cultural descriptions that make up the core of her ethnographic practice" ("Decolonizing Ethnography," 246). Fischer-Hornung ("'Keep Alive the Powers of Africa'") discusses how the African diasporic culture of the Caribbean influenced Hurston's career. Bartkowski explores Hurston's approach to issues of authority and gender, as well as the tension created in the text between researcher and traveler (*Travelers, Immigrants, Inmates: Essays in Estrangement* [Minneapolis: University of Minnesota Press, 1995]).

22. Hemenway, *Zora Neale Hurston,* 248, 249. Hemenway also criticizes the text's "naive" political analysis (249). Several critics argue that Hurston's portrayal of Haitian politics in *Tell My Horse* suggests her support of U.S. imperialism following the U.S. occupation of Haiti. See Dorothea Fischer-Hornung, "An Island Occupied: The U.S. Marine Occupation of Haiti in Zora Neale Hurston's *Tell My Horse* and Katherine Dunham's *Island Possessed,*" in *Holding Their Own: Perspectives on the Multi-ethnic Literatures of the United States,* ed. Dorothea Fischer-Hornung and Heike Raphael-Hernandez (Tübingen: Stauffenburg Verlag, 2000), 153–68; J. Michael Dash, *Haiti and the United States: National Stereotypes and the Literary Imagination* (Houndmills: Macmillan, 1988); John Carlos Rowe, *Literary Culture and U.S. Imperialism: From the Revolution to World War II* (New York: Oxford University Press, 2000); and Annette Trefzer "Possessing the Self: Caribbean Identities in Zora Neale Hurston's *Tell My Horse,*" *African American Review* 34, no. 2 (2000): 299–312.

23. Hurston, *Tell My Horse,* 17.

24. Hurston, *Dust Tracks on a Road,* 286.

25. Hemenway, *Zora Neale Hurston,* 286. Ann Rayson suggests that "through style alone [Hurston] can get away with saying things for which a straight [black] conservative . . . could never be forgiven." Rayson views the ending of *Dust Tracks on a Road* as "both naively ridiculous and camp in a finely ironic self-parody" ("Dust Tracks on a Road: Zora Neale Hurston and the Form of Black Autobiography," *Negro American Literature Forum* 7, no. 2 [Summer 1973]: 39). Hemenway also notes that Hurston's irony loses its edge in the idealistic final sentences of the text, where she imagines an "integrated barbecue in the great beyond" (*Zora Neale Hurston,* 286).

26. Zora Neale Hurston, *Their Eyes Were Watching God* (Philadelphia: J. B. Lippincott, 1937), 209.

27. Hurston, *Tell My Horse,* 17–18.

28. Patricia A. Schechter, *Ida B. Wells-Barnett and American Reform, 1880–1930* (Chapel Hill: University of North Carolina Press, 2001), 125. For discussion of how the charge of rape was used to mask the racist agenda of segregation and lynching, see Patricia A. Schechter, "Unsettled Business: Ida B. Wells against Lynching, or, How Antilynching Got Its Gender," in *Under Sentence of Death: Lynching in the South,* ed. W. Fitzhugh Brundage (Chapel Hill: University of North Carolina Press, 1997), 292–317.

29. Wiegman, *American Anatomies,* 84.

30. Mason Stokes, *The Color of Sex: Whiteness, Heterosexuality, and the Fictions of White Supremacy* (Durham: Duke University Press, 2001), 101.
31. Hurston, *Tell My Horse,* 19.
32. Wiegman, *American Anatomies,* 67.
33. Hurston, *Tell My Horse,* 19–20.
34. Eve E. Dunbar notes the "lack of diasporic community building" in the text and critiques Hurston's evaluation of racial progress in the Caribbean for the way that it "establish[es] U.S.-based racial politics as the model for the rest of the black diaspora" (*Black Regions of the Imagination: African American Writers between the Nation and the World* [Philadelphia: Temple University Press, 2013], 49, 50).
35. Mary Louise Pratt, *Imperial Eyes: Travel Writing and Transculturation,* 2nd ed. (New York: Routledge, 2008), 102; Bartkowski, *Travelers, Immigrants, Inmates,* 35.
36. Hurston, *Tell My Horse,* 75–76.
37. Meehan, "Decolonizing Ethnography," 269; Dunbar, *Black Regions of the Imagination,* 55, 56. Dunbar concedes, however, that because issues of race, gender, and nationalism "coexist" in the text "without ever becoming fully cohesive," we can "read Hurston's work in dynamic ways that challenge a variety of status quo assumptions regarding race, gender, nationalism, art, and science in the early- to mid-twentieth century" (17).
38. Hurston, *Tell My Horse,* 22, 24, 27–29.
39. Ibid., 47, 75.
40. Zora Neale Hurston, "The Gilded Six-Bits," *Story* 3 (August 1933): 60–70.
41. Hurston, *Dust Tracks on a Road,* 253.
42. Hurston, *Tell My Horse,* 78–81, 77, 29.
43. Plant, *Zora Neale Hurston,* 72.
44. Shealeen Meaney, "'In My American Fashion': National Identity, Race, and Gender Tourism in Select Works by Zora Neale Hurston, Grace Seton-Thompson, and Zatella Turner," *Women's Studies: An Inter-disciplinary Journal* 38, no. 7 (2009): 782, 783.
45. Hurston also adopts a relatively objective and detached perspective at strategic moments in her discussions of voodoo in *Tell My Horse,* particularly when she describes potentially dangerous ceremonies, and we find a similar perspective in her 1931 long essay "Hoodoo in America" (*Journal of American Folklore* 44, no. 174 [1931]: 317–417), a discussion of African magic practices and beliefs in the southeastern United States. Meaney notes that Hurston may avoid "too close an association with the local women" in *Tell My Horse* because it might "undermine the status of professional outsider which opens up the space for her intellectual and personal development" ("In My American Fashion," 783).
46. Hurston, *Tell My Horse,* 143–45, 150–51, 153.
47. Harold Courlander, "Witchcraft in the Caribbean Islands," *Saturday Review,* October 15, 1938, 6–7.
48. Review of *Tell My Horse, New Republic,* December 7, 1938, 155.
49. Alain Locke, "The Negro: 'New' or Newer," *Opportunity,* February 1939, 38.
50. M. Genevieve West, *Zora Neale Hurston and American Literary Culture* (Gainesville: University Press of Florida, 2005), 138–39.
51. Carter G. Woodson, review of *Tell My Horse, Journal of Negro History* 24, no.1 (January 1939): 116.
52. Bartkowski, *Travelers, Immigrants, Inmates,* 40, 35.
53. Ibid., 47.

54. Helmers and Mazzeo, "Introduction," 267; Pratt, *Imperial Eyes.*
55. Radhika Mohanram, *Black Body: Women, Colonialism, and Space* (Minneapolis: University of Minnesota Press, 1999), 16.
56. Hurston, *Tell My Horse,* 35, 36.
57. *Zora Neale Hurston: A Life in Letters,* 376.
58. Dunbar, *Black Regions of the Imagination,* 52.
59. Hurston, *Tell My Horse,* 184–87, 167, 169 (emphasis added).
60. *Zora Neale Hurston: A Life in Letters,* 391.
61. Hemenway, *Zora Neale Hurston,* 213.
62. *Zora Neale Hurston: A Life in Letters,* 391.
63. Hurston, *Tell My Horse,* 189 (emphasis added).
64. Hurston, *Dust Tracks on a Road,* 205.
65. Hurston, *Tell My Horse,* 191, 206.
66. Ibid., 199, 206. Although the more thrilling aspects of Hurston's narrative, such as her encounters with secret societies, were used to promote the book as "an exploitative adventure for sightseers" (West, *Zora Neale Hurston,* 128), an October 23, 1938, *New York Times Book Review* of the text plays up Hurston's adventures while at the same time praising the book's stylistic restraint. The reviewer emphasizes Hurston's encounter with a Zombie, her participation in the wild pig hunt, and her close encounters with secret societies such as the Cochon Gris, but notes that despite all of this, the book is written with "level-headed balance, with no sensationalism, in a style which is vivid, sometimes lyrical, occasionally strikingly dramatic, yet simple and unstrained" ("Lore of Haiti," *New York Times Book Review,* October 23, 1938, 12).
67. Hurston, *Tell My Horse,* 210, 221.
68. *Zora Neale Hurston: A Life in Letters,* 384, 385.
69. Hurston, *Tell My Horse,* 221.
70. Shealeen Meaney suggests that "the risks inherent in the search [for knowledge about Zombies] become essential to Hurston's cultivation of the adventurous traveler identity. Significantly, [it] is the *risk,* not the *struggle* that she foregrounds." Furthermore, "the hardships of the body . . . are . . . represented as evidence of Hurston's commitment to the 'truth' " (" 'In My American Fashion,' " 777, 779).
71. Hurston, *Tell My Horse,* 223–24, 221.
72. Wendy Dutton, "The Problem of Invisibility: Voodoo and Zora Neale Hurston," *Frontiers* 13, no. 2 (1993): 133.
73. Fischer-Hornung, "Keep Alive the Powers of Africa," 352.
74. Alasdair Pettinger, " 'Talking Patriots': Americans, Haiti and 'The Negro Problem,' " *Studies in Travel Writing* 1, no. 1 (Spring 1997): 156, 157.
75. Hurston, *Tell My Horse,* 234, 221.
76. Ibid., 259, 266, 258.
77. Zora Neale Hurston, "Eatonville When You Look at It," in *Go Gator and Muddy the Water: Writings by Zora Neale Hurston from the Federal Writers' Project,* ed. Pamela Bordelon (New York: Norton, 1999), 124, 125.
78. Ulysses Lee, "New Negro Americana," *Opportunity,* August 1938, 240.
79. Locke, "The Negro," 39.
80. Lee, "New Negro Americana," 239, 240.
81. Bartkowski, *Traveler, Immigrants, Inmates,* 47.

EPILOGUE

1. Richard Wright, "The Ethics of Living Jim Crow" (1937), in *The Norton Anthology of African American Literature,* ed. Henry Louis Gates Jr. and Nellie Y. McKay (New York: Norton, 2004), 1418.
2. Brian Norman and Piper Kendrix Williams, "To Lie, Steal, and Dissemble: The Cultural Work of the Literature of Segregation," in *Representing Segregation: Toward an Aesthetics of Living Jim Crow, and Other Forms of Racial Division,* ed. Brian Norman and Piper Kendrix Williams (Albany: SUNY Press, 2010), 2.
3. Gary Orfield and Erica Frankenberg with Jongyeon Ee and John Kuscera, "*Brown* at 60: Great Progress, a Long Retreat and an Uncertain Future," the Civil Rights Project / *Proyecto Derechos Civiles,* UCLA, May 15, 2014, http://civilrightsproject.ucla.edu.
4. See Ta-Nehisi Coates, "The Case for Reparations," *Atlantic,* June 2014, www.theatlantic.com.
5. Martha J. Cutter, "White versus Black Justice," OUPblog, November 4, 2013, http://blog.oup.com.
6. Ida B. Wells, *Crusade for Justice: The Autobiography of Ida B. Wells,* ed. Alfreda M. Duster (Chicago: University of Chicago Press, 1970), 187.

INDEX

Page numbers in *italics* refer to illustrations.

GARY TOTTEN was born in Cranbrook, British Columbia, and grew up in the nearby town of Jaffray. He received a BA and MA from Brigham Young University in Provo, Utah, and a PhD from Ball State University. He is the editor of *Memorial Boxes and Guarded Interiors: Edith Wharton and Material Culture* (2007) and coeditor of the forthcoming volume *Politics, Mobility, and Identity in Travel Writing* from Routledge. He has published over twenty articles on late nineteenth- and early twentieth-century U.S. literature, culture, and travel writing. He is professor and chair of English at North Dakota State University and the editor-in-chief of *MELUS: Multi-Ethnic Literature of the United States.* He lives in Moorhead, Minnesota, with his wife, Christine, and enjoys hearing from his three children, Nicolas, Peter, and Anne, who have left home to pursue their own adventures.